CREATION &
CONFEDERATION

The Living History of the Iroquois

Darren Bonaparte

THE WAMPUM CHRONICLES

Ahkwesáhsne Mohawk Territory
2006

Illustration credits:
Dave Fadden: Cover, 12, 46, 112
Natasha Smoke-Santiago: 17, 53, 87
Teyowisonte Deer: 69, 136
Curtis Mitchell, Jr.: 101
Darren Bonaparte: 13, 20, 36, 40, 58, 71, 78
New York State Museum: 113, 115, 121, 124

For information about permissions, or to inquire about bulk purchases of this title, address all correspondence to either of the following mailing addresses or via the internet:

The Wampum Chronicles
c/o The Mohawk Territory of Akwesasne
P.O. Box 459, 1 Angus George Boulevard, Akwesasne QC H0M 1A0 (Canada)
P.O. Box 1026, Akwesasne NY 12655 (USA)
Phone: 613-575-9985
E-mail: wampumchronicles@hotmail.com
Website: www.wampumchronicles.com

First published 2006 by The Wampum Chronicles.
First printing, 2006.

Library of Congress Control Number: 2008910519

ISBN 0-9739322-0-1

ACKNOWLEDGEMENTS

I am indebted to the many writers living and dead whose words I have gathered here in this book. One of them, Dr. William N. Fenton, passed away as I wrote it. This book is dedicated to all those who have added to the Iroquoian literature over the years…and to those who kept alive the oral traditions that inspired these writings.

Niawenkowa to Mohawk storytellers Sakokwenonkwas (Tom Porter) and Tekaronianeken (Jake Swamp) for sparking my interest in the creation story and Peacemaker legend many years ago, and to the many people who have shared their knowledge and insights about our traditional teachings over the years.

Niawenkowa to some of the modern keepers of the Rotinonhsón:ni literary tradition—Dr. Taiaiake Alfred, Teyowisonte Deer, Kahente Doxtater, Michael Galban, Gregg Powless, Todd Powless, Dr. Brian Rice, and Eric Thompson—for sharing copies of old sources, providing proper Mohawk spellings, reading drafts of the manuscript, and giving me honest and productive feedback.

Niawenkowa to all those who helped me bring the manuscript into its final form: Dr. Nadine Jennings of SUNY Canton, who reviewed the manuscript for errors; Natasha Smoke-Santiago, who created several original illustrations; Curtis Mitchell, Jr., who loaned me one of his sketches; Dave Fadden, who provided the cover art; and Gisele Poirier, for bringing the whole thing together for publication with style and class.

Finally, I would like to thank my family and friends for all of the support and encouragement they've given me throughout the writing of this book.

Darren Bonaparte

TABLE OF CONTENTS

Blessed are the peacemakers,
for they shall be called sons of God.

Matthew 5:9

INTRODUCTION

I f there is one symbol by which the *Rotinonhsón:ni*[1] are most well-known, it is the wampum belt that honors a founder of our confederacy, an Onondaga man of many sorrows named *Aionwà:tha*.

Aionwà:tha's wampum belt was the inspiration for the flag flying proudly from one end of Iroquoia to the other. This iconic image—a white chain of four squares and a pine tree on a purple background—could not have been better conceived by a Madison Avenue advertising firm, for it is universally accepted by the people it represents. It is sewn in our clothing, tattooed on our skin, and incorporated into the logo of practically every company and sports team.

It is the meaning of the belt that resonates with the Rotinonhsón:ni. It represents not only *The Great Law of Peace* that unified the Five Nations, but an imagined "golden age" before European contact—as well as the hope that not all of our glory days are behind us.

Aionwà:tha's story, the epic of confederation, is essentially a sequel to the Rotinonhsón:ni creation story. Told in sequence, there is no better introduction to our cultural world.

When the stories first caught my interest, I asked the question that many ask: *Which of the written versions is considered "definitive?"* I was told that there really is no such thing. Instead, there are a number of versions recorded at various times throughout history, sometimes in the native tongue, sometimes in translation, each of them forming a part of the overall tradition. While some have sought in vain for just such a definitive version, the true strength of these cultural epics is their variety. This means they've been fully digested by wide range of people, and are expressing themselves through us in all our diversity. What would it say about our confederacy if we all told the same story the exact same way?

This is not to say that there never was a definitive version of either of these stories. At one time, there may well have been. I have no doubt that both are based on true events. (The world was created, and I'm pretty sure the confederacy was too.) As you read this book, you will see that an evolution occurred with each new telling that reflected the times of each particular storyteller. I present several versions of the confederation epic, some in their entirety, in the order in which they appeared. The length of some quotes goes against the grain of modern conventions, but I felt the rarity of the sources warranted the extra attention given them.

That being said, this is not an exhaustive collection of all the known versions, nor a point-by-point comparison of each of them. For the confederation epic, I focus mainly on the characterization of Aionwà:tha and Tekanawí:ta, the principals actors of the drama, and how their roles evolved over time.

The chronological focus of this book is essentially "pre-contact," but the sources I draw from are "post-contact." The earliest of these is over three and a half centuries old, recorded by a Dutch settler. There is no doubt that the experience of colonization colored the way each of our chroniclers saw the past, whether native or colonist, just as our own experiences color the way we look back on history today. Nevertheless, a chronological focus on the colonial era will have to await another book—its unmistakable shadow will have to suffice for this one.

You will notice that my use and definition of "living history" throughout the text is slightly different than the way historical re-enactors employ the term. My concept of living history goes beyond getting dressed up in period clothing, although it can include that if one is so inclined.

As I have come to understand it, a nation or people with a *living culture* also have a *living history*. A living history is one that evolves with a people as time goes by, getting more complex as we need it to be. An example of this is the way a modern version of the creation story explains how Europeans, Africans, and Asians were created, when the original story only mentioned Native Americans. A living history is free to incorporate new information about the past. It may not bear any resemblance to a more "empirical" history recognized by scholars, but it contains a wealth of information on other levels.

That is not to say that a living history is simply an oral tradition, or, as the federal government's lawyer fighting your land claim might suggest, historical revisionism. A living history can incorporate information found in historical documents, museum collections, and archaeological artifacts, in addition to that which is conveyed from tribal elders. The common wisdom says our ancestors were not a literate people, capturing their words only in petroglyphs and wampum belts, yet the texts I present say otherwise. Somehow, the Iroquois of old made sure their stories made it to print, either by telling them to some European scribe, or by learning to read and write themselves. Their efforts allow us to "time travel" to recover details of the story that may have been lost along the way. Reading their words, you will find that something of their spirit and attitude comes through—something that isn't hard to recognize as our own.

Ultimately, a living history is one that has come to life in the minds of the people, an inner reality in which our ancestors continue to guide us. Eventually their story becomes our story—and goes on and on forever.

I

THE AGE OF CREATION

1

THE VALLEY OF THE GREAT TURTLE

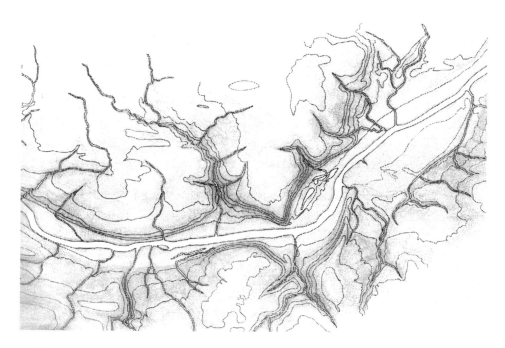

Our journey through history begins in the heart of the ancient homelands of the *Kanien'kehá:ka*, "the people of the place of flint." We're sitting on the grass at *Kana'tsioharé:ke*, "the place of the clean pot," listening to a Mohawk elder as he recounts the story of creation for a gathering of people. He tells the tale against the backdrop of a steep canyon wall that rises more than 500 feet above the nearby Mohawk River, *Tenonanatsieh*, "the river flowing through mountains."

The story he tells is as old as the hills. Somewhere along this river in 1644, another Mohawk storyteller told a similar tale to Dutch colonist Johannes Megapolensis, which he recorded in his *Account of the Mohawk Indians*:

The other day an old woman came to our house, and told my people that her forefathers had told her "that Tharonhij-Jagon, that is, God, once went out walking with his brother, and a dispute arose between them, and God killed his brother." I suppose this fable took its rise from Cain and Abel. They have a droll theory of the Creation, for they think that a pregnant woman fell down from heaven, and that a tortouise, (tortoises are plenty and large here, in this country, two, three and four feet long, some with two heads, very mischievous and addicted to biting) took this pregnant woman on its back, because every place was covered with water; and that the woman sat upon the tortoise, groped with her hands in the water, and scraped together some of the earth, whence it finally happened that the earth was raised above the water. They think that there are more worlds than one, and that we came from another world.

The Mohawk Indians are divided into three tribes, which are called *Ochkori, Anaware, Oknaho*, that is, the Bear, the Tortoise and the Wolf. Of these, the Tortoise is the greatest and most prominent; and they boast that they are the oldest descendents of the woman before mentioned.[2]

It is not surprising that our ancient creation story describes a great turtle rising up from beneath the waters to form the world we know, for this is literally what happened.

For thousands of years, a massive glacier covered much of North America. Eventually it began to melt, leaving a vast body of water over what is now Lake Ontario and the surrounding lands: basically, what would in due time become the homelands of the "Iroquoian" peoples. This body of water drained to the east through what eventually become the Mohawk River, later joining another body of melted glacial ice where we now find Lake Champlain and the Hudson River. As Codman Hislop described it in *The Mohawk*:

The Mohawk gateway to the west was thrown open when the last ice sheet retreated far enough to the north to allow the impounded waters of Lake Iroquois to spill east across the great plateau at what is now Little Falls, New York. What geologists call the Rome River, a pre-glacial stream, had once flowed west from this high land before it disappeared. With the rush of water to the east across this spillway the pre-glacial valley of the Mohawk was filled with roar and rush and the grinding of ice. The flood poured east, cutting out the farmed, green reaches of today, tearing down not only the rock gate at Little Falls, but another stone barrier at what is called "The Noses," huge projections which the quiet river now divides a few miles west of the village of Fonda.[3]

In time, the ice sheath receded northward and this ancient *Lake Iroquois* began to drain through the St. Lawrence River, and the Mohawk River became, in Hislop's words, "a quieter stream."

The Noses he referred to are none other than the massive rock prominences known as *Anthony's Nose* and *Little Nose*. Anthony's Nose is just east of Kana'tsiohará:ke. Little Nose is directly south of it, on the opposite side of the Mohawk River.

It was our modern Mohawk storyteller who first suggested that Anthony's Nose looked a lot like the nose of a giant turtle. Indeed, if seen from above, or even by looking at a topographical map, one can see that the entire area within that particular oxbow of the Mohawk River, from Palatine Bridge to Fonda, is in the shape of a great turtle. And as it happens, this great turtle was created from a massive flood of water that staggers the imagination.

Archaeologists tell us that in the late 1600's, the Mohawk turtle clan villages were located to the east of Anthony's Nose, the bear clan being west of that marker, the wolves several miles further to the west. At an even earlier time, from the 1580's until the second decade of the 1600's, the Mohawk villages were located at various places on the turtle's shell.[4] It is not surprising that the great turtle would figure so prominently in our cosmology, as evidenced by the quote from Megapolensis. Out of his own ignorance, he chuckled at this "droll theory of Creation," but today we realize that our ancestors actually had a fairly advanced understanding of how their landscape came to be created.

Eventually this "Great Turtle Island" would come to represent not only this particular bluff along the Mohawk River, but probably the vast Adirondack mountain range north of it, as well as the entire continent of North America. The great turtle figures prominently in the creation stories of many tribes, but I know of only one place where you can actually "see" the turtle, and that's in our ancient homeland.

Some say we shouldn't take this story so literally, that we should just celebrate its creative imagery. I tried my best to keep that in my mind as I wrote this book, even when a massive tsunami struck southeast Asia, killing hundreds of thousands—and proving for all time that we really do live on the backs of great turtles, and do so at their leisure.

2

Who Was *Sky Woman?*

Nine years after Megapolensis recorded his account of the Mohawk creation story, Adriaen Cornelissen van der Donck captured another version, this one with an interesting variation. We find it in his *Description of New Netherland* (1653).

They say that before the world and the mountains, humans, and animals had come into existence God was with the woman who dwells with him, and no one knows when that was or where they had come from. Water was all there was or at any rate water covered and overran everything. Even if an eye had existed at that time it could not have seen anything but water wherever it might have been, for all was water or covered by water. What then happened, they say, was that the aforementioned beautiful woman or idol descended from heaven into the water. She was gross and big like a woman who is pregnant of more than one child. Touching down gently, she did not sink deep, for at once a patch of land began to emerge under her at the spot where she had come down, and there she came to rest and remained. The land waxed greater so that some areas became visible around the place where she sat, like someone standing on a sandbar in three or four feet of water while it ebbs away and eventually recedes so far that it leaves him entirely on dry land. That is how it went with the descended goddess, they say and believe, the land ever widening around her until its edge disappeared from view. Gradually grass and other vegetation sprang up and in time also fruit-bearing, and other trees, and from this, in brief, the whole globe came into being such as it appears to this day.

Now whether the world you speak of and originally came from was then created as well, we are unable to say. At the time when all that had been accomplished the high personage went into labor and, being confined, gave birth to three different creatures: the first was in every respect like a deer as they are today, the second resembled a bear, and the third a wolf. The woman suckled those creatures to maturity and remained on earth for a considerable time during which she cohabited with each of the said animals and was delivered a number of times of various creatures in multiple births. Thus were bred all humans and animals of the several kinds and species that can still be seen in our day. In due course they began to segregate according, to the families and species still existing, both from an innate urge and for the sake of propriety. When all those things had thus been disposed and made self-perpetuating the universal mother ascended again to heaven rejoicing at having accomplished her task. There she continues to dwell forever, finding her entire happiness and delight in keeping and fostering the supreme Lord's love for her. To that she is devoted and from it derives her complete enjoyment and satisfaction; therefore, God vouchsafes her his fondest love and highest esteem. Here below meanwhile humans and animals of all the various species that were the result of miscegenation increase and multiply, as does all creation the way we find it still. That is why human beings of whatever condition still exhibit the innate characters of one or other of the three animals mentioned, for they are either timid and harmless in the nature of deer, or vindictive, cruel, bold, and direct in the nature of bears, or bloodthirsty, greedy, subtle, and treacherous like wolves.[5]

Van der Donck's version of the creation story leaves out the "Turtle Island" imagery but retains the celestial woman who falls to earth and brings forth life, in this case by giving birth to a deer, a bear, and a wolf. Other versions, such as those told by elders today, say that Sky Woman gave birth not to three animals, but to a daughter who would later give birth to twin sons, variously known as Sapling and Flint or *Teharonhiawá:kon* and *Tawískaron*. (Some say Sky Woman herself gave birth to the twin sons.) These twins created many of the things on earth but eventually had a great battle to determine who would rule the world.

Teharonhiawá:kon is of course the *Tharonhij-Jagon* that Megapolensis's elderly Mohawk informant mentioned, the very same "God" who went out walking with his brother and killed him over a dispute. Megapolensis assumed that this was just a garbled version of the Cain and Abel story from the Bible that somehow found its way into the Mohawk legends, perhaps from earlier contacts with Europeans, but today we are more inclined to recognize a universal duality going on in this story rather than just a case of cultural contamination.

Perhaps the identities of Sky Woman and her battling progeny aren't quite as mysterious as all of this may seem. Perhaps we're really talking about real, flesh and blood people, our own ancestors. Sky Woman may have been the original woman who led us to our historic place on the turtle's shell, and Sapling and Flint may have been her sons or grandsons, perhaps leaders of rival factions. Maybe she isn't just one woman, but a symbolic representation of the women who were in control back then. Her giving birth to various animals in the van der Donck version may simply explain the origin of various clans.

An archaeologist who has studied the Mohawk Valley believes that when our ancient ancestors established themselves there, they already had a matrilineal society.[6] The Iroquoian mix of horticulture, hunting, and fishing required a more sophisticated social and political structure than your typical roving band of male-dominated hunters. The prominence of a "Sky Woman" in our creation story not only gives our matrilineal society an ancient pedigree, but a sense of divinity. Who can argue with something sent from heaven?

3

HAVE ASTRONOMERS DISCOVERED SKY WORLD?

Johannes Megapolensis, the Dutch colonist who captured the first known Mohawk creation story in 1644, probably would have been amazed that the Mohawks would continue to believe in it for more than three and a half centuries, but that is indeed what has happened.

The story of creation, which has often been called by the more formal name of *The Myth of the Earth Grasper,* is still the foundation of not

only traditional Mohawk beliefs, but those of our brother Iroquoians, just as it was in the time of Megapolensis. It has evolved over time, as all great traditions do, but there are many important aspects of it that have survived virtually intact over the centuries. One of them is the central premise that life on earth has extraterrestrial origins. As Megapolensis said:

> They think that there are more worlds than one, and that we came from another world.[7]

That's right, an integral part of Iroquoian spiritual beliefs is that life on earth was in part seeded from another planet—a place known to us as *Karonhià:ke,* or Sky World. It's one of those areas where our traditional teachings agree with those of other peoples, for it was almost universal among the ancients that beings from the heavens were involved in creation.

For years, these "heavenly beings" were the basis of all of the world's religions, but today we only associate the concept with one thing: little green men from Mars.

We owe this in part to Erich von Däniken, whose pseudo-scientific book *Chariots of the Gods? Unsolved Mysteries of the Past* reintroduced the concept of "ancient astronauts" into the public consciousness in 1967. Ancient astronauts have become a staple plot device of science fiction movies since then, but few scientists take the idea seriously. As mysterious as the Great Pyramids of Giza are, there is no question that *men* made them, not alien gods, although their makers certainly had a rich cultural world that spoke of celestial gods and goddesses—the *Star Wars* of their time.

One scientist who does take the ancient astronauts seriously is Zecharia Sitchin, the Israeli scholar who authored *The Twelfth Planet*, *The Stairway to Heaven*, *The Wars of Gods and Men*, *The Lost Realm*, *When Time Began*, and *The Cosmic Code*. These books are collectively known as *The Earth Chronicles*.

Sitchin's take on the ancient astronauts scenario is much more detailed and involved than von Däniken's work, but it is not without its share of skeptics. At the heart of his theory is the belief that the ancient Sumerians knew of a tenth member of our solar system—the planet *Nibiru*, the birthplace of their gods. Based on his reading of ancient Mesopotamian texts, Sitchin says that this "planet of the gods" has a massive orbit that brings it around the sun once every 3,600 years, and whenever it comes closer to the inner planets, it usually wreaks havoc. This was the cause of the great flood talked about in the biblical story of Noah's ark.

Although this planet's orbit takes it quite a distance from the warmth of the sun, it apparently has a means of generating enough heat of its own to support life. Sitchin says that the beings who lived on this planet—the *Anunnaki*, or "Those who from heaven to Earth came" — traveled here to mine for gold, but quickly grew tired of their toil. A member of the Anunnaki royal family, a scientist named *Ea*, noticed that the planet already had a creature similar to themselves, and suggested a solution to the labor crisis: genetically engineer a "hybrid" from the DNA of these primitive beings and the gods themselves.

Once perfected, the hybrids were immediately put to work to relieve the gods. Eventually they made enough of these new hybrids that the gods began to take some of them as wives. The noise from all of this debauchery angered Ea's brother, *Enlil*, who decided that it was time for the end of this new creation. When the Planet of the Gods came around for another visit, its gravitational pull caused a massive flood on earth that wiped out most of humanity. Fortunately, Ea was able to prevent mankind's total destruction by advising a chosen few to build an ark and save themselves.

If this sounds similar to the Book of Genesis in the Bible, it's because Genesis is a regeneration of these earlier Near Eastern tales. *Yahweh* (Jehovah) is an amalgamation of these two ancient Sumerian gods, Ea and Enlil. (Since the ancient Jews were nomadic, they had to travel light, both physically and spiritually, and that meant no idol worship and only one deity!)

I mention Sitchin's theory because in the original Sumerian legends about the creation of man, they speak of the new worker being fashioned from clay mixed with the blood of a god. Life is then "breathed into" the new creation, which Sitchin interprets as the mixing of Anunnaki DNA with that of our evolutionary predecessors. It is reminiscent of how man was created in modern versions of our own creation story, such as the one found in the North American Indian Travelling College's *Traditional Teachings* (1984):

> When Teharonhiawako created all the waters, plants, trees, and animals of the world, he decided that he should create a being in his likeness from the natural world.
>
> He wanted this being to have a superior mind so it would have the responsibility of looking after his creations. Then he decided that it would be better if he created more than one being and give to each similar instructions and see if over a period of time, they would carry them through.

The first being Teharonhiawako made was from the bark of a tree; the second from the foam of the great salt water, the third from the black soil...

Now Teharonhiawako thought to himself, it is getting towards the end of the day and I have created three beings, since everything on this world exists in cycles of four, I will create one more being. Thus he again looked for something different within the natural world and this time he found some reddish-brown earth. With this he again combined other elements from the land and created a human form. When he finished he observed that his form blended very well with the natural surroundings, especially against the setting sun, which gave the form a reddish color.[8]

Are these "battling brothers," the great flood, and the creation of man from clay just more examples of universal human archetypes, or could there be a more tangible connection between Ea and Enlil of the Sumerians and Teharonhiawá:kon and Tawískaron of our own creation story? It was something I thought I would never know the answer to.

That all changed on July 29th, 2005, when a NASA website announced some surprising news:

"It's definitely bigger than Pluto." So says Dr. Mike Brown of the California Institute of Technology who announced today the discovery of a new planet in the outer solar system.

The planet, which hasn't been officially named yet, was found by Brown and colleagues using the Samuel Oschin Telescope at Palomar Observatory near San Diego. It is currently about 97 times farther from the sun than Earth, or 97 Astronomical Units (AU). For comparison, Pluto is 40 AU from the sun.

This places the new planet more or less in the Kuiper Belt, a dark realm beyond Neptune where thousands of small icy bodies orbit the sun. The planet appears to be typical of Kuiper

Belt objects—only much bigger. Its sheer size in relation to the nine known planets means that it can only be classified as a planet itself, Brown says.[9]

One would expect that Zecharia Sitchin would be thrilled to hear that the existence of his "Planet of the Gods" had been confirmed by science, but as he stated on his website, he didn't believe this "icy rock" was the same planet:

> So is it Nibiru? Have astronomers now found the planet from which, according to my understanding of Mesopotamian and biblical texts and illustrations, astronauts had come to Earth some 450,000 years ago?
>
> Based on the sketchy information so far available, the answer is No.
>
> This regrettable answer stems, first of all, from comparing the information released regarding the new object and the ancient data concerning Nibiru. The latter was described as a radiating planet (i.e. one that has its own heat source and atmosphere), a planet that sustains life, home planet of the Anunnaki ("Those who from heaven to Earth came") — the biblical Nefilim…It was not an "icy rock" in the Kuiper belt.[10]

It seems doubtful that NASA is contemplating a manned space mission to the outer solar system to see if God is home, so it may be some time before we find out if this "tenth planet" is Sitchin's Nibiru, the Planet of the Gods—or Karonhià:ke, the Sky World of the Iroquois.

4

THE SEARCH FOR NEW WORLD SYMBOLS IN OLD WORLD MYTHOLOGY

The search for possible links between the legends of the New World and the Old is nothing new. A Jesuit priest by the name of Father Joseph Francois Lafitau, who served in Kahnawà:ke from 1712 to 1717, sought connections between Iroquois and "classical" mythology. He detailed his findings in *Mœurs des sauvages amériquains, comparées aux mœurs des premiers temps,* published in 1724. A translation of this work, *Customs of the American Indians Compared with the Customs of Primitive Times,* was published in two volumes by William Fenton and Elisabeth L. Moore in 1974 and 1977.

Lafitau recounts the story of creation, presumably shared with him by his Iroquois flock:

> Here is the story that the Iroquois tell of their origin and that
> of the earth. In the beginning, there were, they say, six men.
> (The peoples of Peru and Brazil agree on a like number.)
> Whence had these men come? That is what they do not know.
> There was as yet no land. They wandered at the will of the
> wind. They had no women and they thought that their race
> was going to perish with them. Finally they learned, I do not
> know where, that there was a woman in the Heavens. They
> held a common council and decided that one of them named
> Hoguaho or the Wolf would go there. The enterprise appeared
> impossible but the birds of the sky in concert together, lifted
> him up there, making a seat for him of their bodies and
> sustaining each other. When he had reached there, he waited
> at the foot of a tree until this woman came out as she was
> accustomed to do, to draw water from a spring near the place
> where he had stopped. The man, who was waiting for her,

entered into conversation with her and made her a present of bear fat which he gave her to eat. A curious woman who likes to talk and receives presents does not long delay in yielding. This one was weak even in heaven itself. She let herself be seduced. The master of the heavens perceived it and, in his wrath, drove her away and hurled her out. When she fell, the turtle received her on his back, on which the otter and the fishes, digging up the clay from the bottom of the water, formed a little island which increased little by little and extended into the form in which we see the earth today. This woman had two children who fought one another. They had unequal arms whose force they did not know. Those of the one were dangerous and the other's could harm no one so that the former (latter) was killed without difficulty.

All other men have their descent from this woman through a long succession of generations, and it is such a singular event as this which has served, they say, as a basis for the division of the three families of the Iroquois and Huron, into those of the Wolf, the Bear and the Turtle which, by their very names, are a living tradition bringing before their eyes the history of the first times.[11]

Lafitau was struck by the story's similarity to Greek mythology:

This tale's absurdity arouses pity although it is no more ridiculous than some of those invented by the Greeks who were such ingenious people. They invented the story of Prometheus' voyage to the heavens when he mounted there to steal fire and that of the rebuilding of the world by Deucalion and Pyrrha who, counselled by the oracles, threw over their heads stones which were converted into men and women, the difference of sex depending only on the hand which had thrown them.

But across this fable, ridiculous as it is, we seem to half-see the truth, in spite of the thick darkness enveloping it. In fact, investigating a little, we distinguish in it the woman in the earthly paradise, the tree of the knowledge of good and evil, the temptation into which she had the misfortune to fall, which some heretics have believed to be a sin of the flesh, (a belief) founded, perhaps, on an alteration by pagan ideas; we discover in it the wrath of God driving our first ancestors from the place delights where he had paced them, (a place) which could be regarded as the sky in comparison with the land which was not to produce by itself anything except thorns and thistles; finally we think that we can see the murder of Abel killed by his brother, Cain.

This fable has also its origin in the mythology of the ancients in which many things taught us by religion are disguised rather than entirely unrecognizable. Homer's story of At's fall is an exact prototype of the Iroquois fable of the woman driven from heaven. At was a goddess, Jupiter's daughter. Her name shows her character which was vice itself. She thought only of doing harm and was capable of nothing else. (She was) odious to Gods and men. Finally, she so irritated Jupiter himself that this god, seizing her by the hair, threw her from the heavens and swore that she should never again set foot there.[12]

Lafitau recognized "Great Turtle Island" as another link to the Old World. In his mind, it evoked the story of Latona, who, when pursued by the serpent Python, "threw herself into the sea where she was received by the Island of Delos. This Island which was at that time swimming between two waters and which had no part in the tumult which had caused the earth to refuse her asylum, appeared suddenly to save her from shipwreck, and was honoured by being the birthplace of Apollo and of Diana."[13]

Lafitau noted that an ancient monument to Harpocrates had him standing on a turtle's back, as did the statue of Venus Urania, or the Celestial Venus:

It would, perhaps, be more natural to think that the ancients wished to indicate by this figure that the Goddess called Venus Urania was the author of the harmony of the world, portrayed by the turtle, the symbol of this harmony, the turtle and Apollo's lyre being the same thing...

...Perhaps they meant also to say that the origin of man who was created on the earth was, nonetheless, divine and came from the heavens.[14]

The turtle also appears in East Indian traditions of the Brahmins. Lafitau notes that their God Vishnu metamorphosed into one:

They say that, by a mountain's fall, the world which could not carry such a heavy burden was going down, little by little, toward the abyss in which it would have perished if Vishnu, the beneficent god, had not metamorphosed himself into a turtle and borne it upon his back.[15]

Finally, Lafitau found the turtle motif in Chinese culture:

The Chinese also make a divinity of the flying dragon which they call the spirit or genius of the air and the mountains and which is seen, in their temples, covered with a turtle shell. They think that this dragon was born of a turtle and say that it is the support of the world which is entirely held up by it. [16]

In a footnote to the translation she and William Fenton published of his work, Elisabeth L. Moore observed of Lafitau, "his work is at its best in some of these myths and in his descriptions of Indian customs. His theoretical religious discussions are so involved and tortuous as to be less interesting."[17] Fenton, while unconvinced of Lafitau's arguments, seemed more appreciative of his methodologies, which he saw as quite advanced for their time:

Although many of his comparisons seem farfetched today, and his inferences from them unjustified, he was more competent than his contemporaries and more mature because of his unique way of utilizing field observations to criticize earlier sources on the Iroquoian peoples and of employing their customs as a means of understanding the nature of antique society and culture.[18]

After his work was published, Lafitau returned to Kahnawà:ke to serve as superior of the mission from 1727 to 1729. He would not be the last scholar to probe Iroquois culture for links to the ancients of the Old World, but he would be one of the last to contribute to scholarship without the competition of our own men of letters. Within a generation of the publication of his great comparative work, some of our own children were taught to read and write. These young scribes would eventually make their own contributions to this literary tradition, but they would be unencumbered by the Eurocentric desire to prove our culture had roots somewhere other than in our own fertile soil.

5

THE IROQUOIS LITERARY TRADITION

The student of Iroquois history is told early on to pay more attention to the oral traditions of our people than to the written literature—"the white man's history books." Just as non-native scholars have dismissed our oral traditions as historically unreliable, our people tend to mistrust what is contained in the documents written by the non-native society. We are reminded that our ancestors didn't have a written language, but relied on the spoken word, pictographic symbols, and wampum belts to communicate and preserve their thoughts.

Of course, it is doubtful that the people who wrote about us fully understood what they were describing. They may have deliberately altered what they saw out of some ulterior motive. But it has been my experience that there is a wealth of historical and cultural information contained within the literature that we would be unwise to dismiss out of hand—especially when we discover the important role our own people had in creating it.

It is a myth that English literacy is a fairly new phenomenon to our people, even though we all know of elders today who are much more comfortable speaking in our language than in English. The truth is, our people have been exposed to "formal" education for about two and a half centuries, although on a very limited basis at first. It hasn't been without controversy. Joseph Brant and Eleazer Williams are examples of Mohawk children who were sent away to an "Indian school" in New England, only to return to their people to become ministers or treaty-signers...or a combination of the two.

Although English literacy offered these individuals access to the non-native world, very few of them used it to leave our people behind. Instead, some of our early scholars used their literacy skills to preserve traditions that they saw as endangered: the language, ceremonies, songs, and legends of their nations. This kind of work began in earnest in the

19th century, which I would describe as the renaissance of Iroquoian literature due to the richness of the material collected at that time.

David Cusick, a Tuscarora, was one native scribe who did extensive work in this regard in the early part of the century. He was followed in the late 1800's by J. N. B. Hewitt, another Tuscarora; Seth Newhouse, a Mohawk; and Ely S. Parker, the Seneca chief who became a general in the Civil War. Parker's nephew Arthur C. Parker continued this tradition into the 20th century. Jesse Cornplanter was another Seneca who not only shared the stories he knew but illustrated them as well. Nor can we forget the countless other Iroquois who may not have written anything themselves, but who willingly shared what they knew with the scholars of their time.

It should not be surprising that so much of the literature concerned itself with our ancient creation story, as this had always been the foundation of our cultural existence, and a natural place to start for someone attempting to explain the way we looked at the world. This was a time of increasing pressures of assimilation, not only by missionary work among the our people, but by non-Indian settlers that engulfed Iroquoia. Nevertheless, oral traditions about creation remained relatively intact.

This is best illustrated by two Onondaga versions, one recorded by Major John Norton in 1816 that was attributed to "an Onondaga Chief of near a hundred years old,"[19] and a longer account, "The Myth of the Earth-Grasper," that J. N. B. Hewitt gathered in the 1890's from John Arthur Gibson, a Seneca condoled as an Onondaga chief. Both go into great detail about the events that happened before Sky Woman fell from Sky World, as well as the conflict between her grandsons, with a remarkable consistency throughout. The same holds true for three other versions that Hewitt found in Mohawk, Seneca, and Onondaga, which we find in *Iroquoian Cosmology*, a two-part monograph published by the Bureau of American Ethnology in 1903 and 1928.[20]

This Iroquois literary tradition continues into modern times. In 1980, the Kahnawake Survival School recounted the story of creation in their Mohawk history textbook, *Seven Generations*.[21] In 1984, the North American Indian Travelling College of Ahkwesáhsne included it in

Traditional Teachings, a collection of Iroquois legends.[22] This was followed in 1998 by Joanne Shenandoah (Oneida) and Douglas M. George (Mohawk) with *Skywoman: Legends of the Iroquois*.[23] More recently, Seneca scholar John Mohawk gave a modernized interpretation in *Iroquois Creation Story: John Arthur Gibson and J. N. B. Hewitt's* Myth of the Earth Grasper (2005).[24]

Many of the people who helped to document the creation story more than a century ago were also consulted about the founding of the league. In their hands, the epic of confederation became a true sequel to the creation story, with themes and symbols carrying over from one to the other.

Arthur C. Parker gives us an example of this in "Emblematic Trees in Iroquoian Mythology," which we find in his *Seneca Myths and Folk Tales*, published in 1923. Parker quotes a Seneca version of the creation story told by Esquire Johnson to Mrs. Asher Wright in 1870:

> She wrote: "—there was a vast expanse of water—Above it was the great blue arch of air but no signs of anything solid. In the clear sky was an unseen floating island sufficiently firm to allow trees to grow upon it, and there were man-beings there. There was one great chief there who gave the law to all the Ongwe or beings on the island. In the center of the island there grew a tree so tall that no one of the beings who lived there could see its top. On its branches flowers and fruit hung all year round. The beings who lived on the island used to come to the tree and eat the fruit and smell the sweet perfume of the flowers. On one occasion the chief desired to that the tree be pulled up. The Great Chief was called to look at the great pit which was to be seen where the tree had stood." The story continues with the usual description of how the sky-mother was pushed into the hole in the sky and fell upon the wings of the waterfowl who placed her on the turtle's back. After this mention of the celestial tree in the same manuscript is the story of the central world-tree. After the birth of twins, Light One and Toad-like (or dark) one, the Light One, also

known as the Good Minded, noticing that there was no light, created the "tree of light." This was a great tree having at its topmost branch a great ball of light. At this time the sun had not been created. It is significant as will appear later that the Good Minded made his tree of light one that brought forth flowers from every branch. After he had gone experimenting and improving the earth "he made a new light and hung it on the neck of a being he called the new light Gaa-gwaa...and instructed its bearer to run his course daily in the heavens." Shortly after he is said to have "dug up the tree of light and looking into the pool of water in which the stump (trunk) had grown he saw the reflection of his own face and thereupon conceived the idea of creating Ongwe and made them both a man and a woman."[25]

Parker relates how "the Great Face, the chief of all False Faces, is said to be the invisible giant that guards the world-tree" planted by the Good Minded:

> He rubs his turtle shell rattle upon it to obtain its power and this he imparts to all the visible faces worn by the Company. In visible token of this belief the members of the Company rub their turtle rattles on pine tree trunks, believing that they become filled with both the earth and sky-power thereby. In the use of the turtle shell rattle there is perhaps a recognition of the connection between the turtle and the world-tree that grows upon the primal turtle's back.[26]

Parker then cites the Peacemaker myth that he gathered at Six Nations:

> In the prologue of the Wampum Code of the Five Nations Confederacy we again find references to a symbolic "great tree." In the code of Dekanawida and with the Five Nations' confederate lords (rodiyaner) "I plant the Tree of the Great Peace. I plant it in your territory,

Adodarho and the Onondaga nation, in the territory of you who are Firekeepers.

"I name the tree the Tree of the Great Long Leaves. Under the shade of this Tree of Peace we spread the soft feathery down of the globe thistle, there beneath the spreading branches of the Tree of Peace."

In the second "law" of the code the four roots of the "tree" are described and the law-giver says, "If any individual or nation outside the Five Nations shall obey the laws of the Great Peace and make their disposition to the Lords of the Confederacy, they may trace the Roots to the Tree and if their minds are clean and obedient—they shall be welcome to take shelter beneath the Tree of the Long Leaves.

"We place at the top of the Tree of the Long Leaves and Eagle who is able to see afar;—he will warn the people."

In another place is the following: "I Dekanawida, and the union lords now uproot the tallest pine tree and into the cavity thereby made we cast all weapons of war. Into the depths of the earth, down into the deep under-earth currents of water flowing to the unknown regions we cast all weapons of strife. We bury them from sight and we plant again the tree. Thus shall the Great Peace, Kayenarhekowa, be established."[27]

The Iroquois would come to invoke similar tree imagery in councils with European powers, as they did in 1684:

"We now plant a Tree who's tops will reach the Sun, and its Branches spread far abroad, so that it shall be seen afar off; & we shall shelter ourselves under it, and live in Peace, without molestation."[28]

Parker points out that tree imagery, earth symbols, and the celestial sky dome were frequently used as decorative patterns on clothing and crafts. Our people have used moose hair, porcupine quill embroidery, and glass beads to incorporate these emblems into the borders of leggings, breechclouts, skirts, and moccasins.

The "uprooted tree" would not be the only carry-over from the creation story, as we will see in later chapters of this work. Pivotal characters manifest themselves as well.

Modern Iroquois storytellers, when giving the short forms of these two legends, usually tell them in sequence, since they flow so naturally together. But in doing so, they leave out the events that occurred between creation and confederation—basically, billions of years of history. Our ancestors had many stories about this period. Fortunate for us, these "forgotten epics" of oral tradition have been preserved for us by the literary tradition.

6

THE CHILDREN OF GAIHONARIOSK

Our creation story celebrates a new beginning, but not necessarily the *only* beginning. The Mohawks of long ago acknowledged that something happened *before* they came to the Valley of the Great Turtle. Father Joseph-Francois Lafitau, a Jesuit priest we encountered in Chapter 4, was told this intriguing tale by Kahnawà:ke Mohawks in the early part of the 18th century:

The Indians, in general, are not unaware that they are foreigners in the lands in which they inhabit at present. They say that they came from afar from the direction of the west, that is to say, from Asia. The Agnie [Mohawk] Iroquois assure us that they wandered a long time under the leadership of a woman named Gaihonariosk. This woman led them all through the north of America. She made them go to the place where the city of Quebec is now situated but, finding the terrain too irregular and the country, perhaps, too disadvantageous because of the cold, she stopped at last at Agnie [Mohawk] where the climate seemed to her more temperate and the lands more suitable for cultivation. She then divided the lands for cultivation and thus founded a colony which has maintained itself ever since. This is the Mohawk's story of their individual origin which they claim is a little different from that of the other four Iroquois nations for they claim not to be included under the name of Agonnonsionni or Builders of Lodges, by which the others are called. I do not know the reason for it [this claim on their part.] The French and the other Indian tribes, however, do not make this distinction and generally, under the name of Iroquois or Agonnonsionni, there are included five peoples who speak as many different dialects of the same language. They are located in that part of New France, situated to the east of the (Great) Lakes and through which the Saint Lawrence River passes. Their land is bordered by New York and the other lands of the English and French. They are divided into upper and lower Iroquois. The upper ones are the Tsonnontouans (Seneca), the Goyogouens (Cayouga), and the Onnontagues (Onondaga). The Lower Iroquois are the Agnie (Mohawk) and the Onnejout (Oneida). These five peoples, in spite of different reasons for jealousy, have always kept united, and to indicate their union they say that they form a single house which we call the Iroquois Longhouse.[29]

This story mentions that the early Mohawks followed a woman named *Gaihonariosk* as far northeast as what is now known as Quebec City before rejecting that land as being unfit for cultivation. They eventually came to the Mohawk Valley, which was much more suitable. Could this Gaihonariosk be the inspiration for "Sky Woman" who landed on the "Great Turtle?" Or is she, like Sky Woman before her, just a symbolic representation of the "matrilineal" nature of the society that remembers her?

Lafitau's writings, like those of his Dutch colleagues, are another example of "hidden knowledge" that doesn't become apparent until a great deal of time has passed. In this case, we have clues not only about the migration of the Mohawks to the valley that bears our name, but to the identity of the so-called "St. Lawrence Iroquoians" that Jacques Cartier encountered at *Stadacona* and *Hochelaga*—today's Quebec City and Montreal. Could these be descendents of Gaihonariosk's band, who perhaps thought the good fishing made up for the bad farming and decided to make a go of it while she led the rest to Mohawk Country?

The question exists today because in the years that followed Cartier's visit, the Stadaconans and Hochelagans disappeared. Where they actually went has been a subject of considerable debate.

There are Mohawks today who insist that the Hochelagans were Mohawks, a position archaeologists agreed with back in the late 1800's, but have long since abandoned. The assumption was that after Cartier's visit, the Hochelagans went south and settled the Mohawk Valley, becoming the historic Mohawks. When archaeologists established our presence in the Mohawk Valley hundreds of years before Cartier's visit, this idea went by the wayside with everyone but the Mohawks.

In a manner of speaking, those Mohawks were right...the people of Hochelaga *were* Mohawks, or at the very least were once a part of the group that later *became* Mohawks. Eventually many of the Hochelagans eventually did end up becoming Mohawk themselves, as this next oral tradition (recorded at Montreal in 1642) suggests:

> The evening of the same day M. de Masionneuve desired to visit the Mountain which gave the island its name, and two old Indians who accompanied him thither, having led him to the top, told him they were of the tribe who had formerly inhabited this country. "We were," they added, "very numerous and all the hills (collines) which you see to the south and east, were peopled. The Hurons drove thence our ancestors, of whom a part took refuge among the Abenakis, others withdrew into the Iroquois cantons, a few remained with our conquerors." They promised Masionneuve to do all they could to bring back their people, "but apparently could not succeed in reassembling the fragments of this dispersed tribe, which doubtless is that of the Iroquois which I have spoken of in my Journal."[30]

To their credit, archaeologists do consider some of these old sources when debating the fate of the St. Lawrence Iroquoians. They've also found pottery and pipes with distinctive "St. Lawrence Iroquoian" features while excavating Abenaki, Huron, and Iroquois sites. Considering that Abenakis and Hurons were absorbed into our population at various times—which could theoretically add even more St. Lawrence Iroquoians to our numbers—the case could be made that if anyone has an ancestral claim to the St. Lawrence River Valley, it would be the "Iroquoians" living on her shores today.

7

THE GOLDEN AGE OF GIANTS, MONSTERS & GRAND CONFEDERACIES

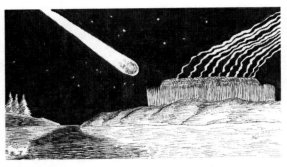

Although relative newcomers to the Iroquois Confederacy, nobody can accuse the Tuscaroras of not taking to the ways of the Longhouse with gusto. Any who doubt this need only consider David Cusick's *Sketches of Ancient History of the Six Nations*, which he wrote in 1825. Cusick was the J. R. R. Tolkien of his day, filling his pages with monsters, giants, and serpents, with the exception that none of his work was fiction, but *history*, at least as the Iroquois saw it. Henry B. Schoolcraft borrowed liberally from Cusick for his 1846 *Notes on the Iroquois*.[31]

Cusick starts off in fine form by presenting the creation story, following it with an amazing chronicle of events that took place long before the Five Nations were united. This is a "golden age" of giants, monsters, and grand confederacies.

> In the ancient days the Great Island appeared upon the big waters, the earth brought forth trees, herbs, vegetables, etc. the creation of the land animals; the Eagwehowewe people were too created, and resided in the northern regions, and after a time some of the people became giants and committed outrages upon the inhabitants, etc. After many years a body of Eagwehoewe people camped on the bank of a majestic stream, and was named *Kanawage*, now St. Lawrence. After a long time a number of foreign people sailed from a port unknown; but unfortunately before reached their destination the winds

drove them contrary; at length their ship wrecked somewhere on the southern part of the Great Island, and many of the crews perished; a few active persons were saved; they obtained some implements and each of them carried them on the summit of a mountain and remained there but a short time the hawks seemed to threaten them, and were compelled to leave the mountain. They immediately selected a place for residence and built a small fortification in order to provide against the attacks of furious beasts; if there should be any made. After many years the foreign people became numerous, and extended their settlements; but afterwards they were destroyed by the monsters that overrun the country…[32]

Cusick tells us the *Eagwehoewe* living on the *Kanawage* had but a short time to enjoy their tranquility before they were invaded by a tribe of giants from the north, the *Ronnongwetowanea.* Then came *Shotyerronsgwea,* "the greatest mischievous person that ever existed on this continent," who tricked his way into their confidence before killing two of their warriors and violating six virgins. This ordeal was followed by an attack of giant beasts.

About this time Big Quisquiss (perhaps the Mammoth) invaded the settlements south of Ontario lake; the furious animal push down the houses and made great disturbance; the people was compelled to flee from the terrible monster; the warriors made opposition but failed; at length a certain chief warrior collected the men from several towns—a severe engagement took place, at last the monster retired, but the people could not remain long without being disturbed; Big Elk invaded the towns: the animal was furious and destroyed many persons; however the men were soon collected—a severe contest ensued and the monster was killed.[33]

Here is where Cusick's tale gets really interesting—that is, if giant animal attacks aren't interesting enough. Cusick offers up this intriguing oral tradition that there was a confederacy long before the Five Nations:

About this time the northern nations formed a confederacy and seated a great council fire on the river St. Lawrence; the northern nations possessed the bank of the great lakes; the countries in the north were plenty of beavers, but the hunters were often opposed by the big snakes. The people live on the south side of the Big Lakes make bread of roots and obtain a kind of potatoes and beans found on the rich soil.

Perhaps about two thousand two hundred years before the Columbus discovered the America, and northern nations appointed a prince, and immediately repaired to the south and visited the great Emperor who resided at the Golden City, a capital of the vast empire. After a time the Emperor built many forts throughout his dominions and almost penetrated the lake Erie; this produced an excitement, the people of the north felt that they would soon be deprived of the country on the south side of the Great Lakes they determined to defend their country against any infringement of foreign people; long bloody wars ensued which perhaps lasted about one hundred years; the people of the north were too skillful in the use of bows and arrows and could endure hardships which proved fatal to a foreign people; at last the northern nations gained the conquest and all the towns and forts were totally destroyed and left them in the heap of ruins.

About this time a great horned serpent appeared on lake Ontario, the serpent produced diseases and many of the people died, but by the aid of thunder bolts the monster was compelled to retire. A blazing star fell into a fort situated on the St. Lawrence and destroyed the people; this event was considered as a warning of their destruction. After a time a war broke out among the northern nations which continued until they had utterly destroyed each other, the island again become in possession of fierce animals.[34]

Our elders never tire of telling us younger people what wimps we are compared to when they were young, but they have nothing on the elders of long ago, who had to deal with a tribe of giants, marauding animals, and a horned serpent. With all due respect, the elders of today wouldn't last a day in such conditions.

It is tempting to speculate as to what Cusick was really describing. It has been suggested that the "shipwreck" mentioned at the beginning may refer to Jacques Cartier's ship getting stuck in ice; and that the tale of the tribe of giants echoes an Anishnabe tradition that they once attacked Montreal Island (site of Hochelaga) and took captives.[35] Cusick suggests the giant "quisquiss" may have been a mammoth, but we recognize it as the Mohawk word for pig, or perhaps a wild boar. The "Big Elk" may have been just that, an abnormally large elk. The "great horned serpent" might just be a normal serpent with his head stuck in some branches. Other elements of the story, like the "Golden City" that served as the capital of a "vast empire," aren't so readily explained.

Cusick seems to suggest that the ancient Iroquoians of the Great Lakes and the St. Lawrence River Valley were a single people, or at least a confederation of related tribes. We know that the Huron have a creation story similar to ours, even though they are far from the Mohawk Valley land formation in the shape of a turtle.

In November 1656, an Oneida delegation to Trois-Rivieres reminded a Huron chief of their ancient ties, as recounted in *The Jesuit Relations*:

> Thou knowest, thou huron, that formerly we comprised but one Cabin and one country. I know not by what accident we became separated. It is time to unite again.[36]

And what of this village on the St. Lawrence that was destroyed by a shooting star? Surely such a calamity would leave evidence, such as a crater or a layer of ash in the ground, but neither of these is known to exist. There is, however, a mysterious hole in the St. Lawrence River between two of Ahkwesáhsne's islands that has always intrigued me. A local fisherman says some pretty big fish live down at the bottom of that hole, which is thought to have been created by the turbulent pre-Seaway current.

Of course, the shooting star may simply have been a metaphor for Jacques Cartier, whose arrival proved to be equally catastrophic for at least one St. Lawrence village, Hochelaga. Being satisfied with that explanation would keep us from having to rent scuba diving equipment and going into that hole to look for a meteor, or whatever it is that's making the fish so big.

Cusick tells us of a "golden age" of Iroquoian unity that came to an end with a heaven-sent cataclysm. This was the beginning of the "dark age" from which the *League of the Longhouse* would one day emerge.

II

THE AGE OF CONFEDERATION

8

DATING THE IROQUOIS CONFEDERACY

No, this isn't a chapter about how to add my good-looking Iroquois cousins to your little black book. It's about another scholarly debate that has dominated Iroquoian studies, much like the mystery of the St. Lawrence Iroquoians. The debate is about when the Five Nations came together as a confederacy and accepted *The Great Law of Peace.*

Iroquoian scholars of the "old school" believe that the Five Nations came together no earlier than a few generations before European contact, whereas the "new breed" of Iroquoianists argue for a much earlier date, say a thousand years ago, based on the testimony of modern Iroquois traditionalists.[37]

Early discussions centered on historical accounts such as one recorded by Reverend John Christopher Pyrlæus, a Moravian minister among the Mohawks in the late 1740's. His source was *Sganarady,* a Mohawk headman known to colonists as David of Scoharie:

> The alliance or confederacy of the Five Nations was estab-
> lished, as near as can be conjectured, one age (or the length of
> one man's life) before the white people (the Dutch) came into
> the country. *Thannawage* was the name of the aged Indian, a
> Mohawk, who first proposed such an alliance.[38]

Pyrlæus also included a familiar list of the league's founders:

> …*Toganawita*, of the Mohawks: *Otatschechta*, of the Oneidas;
> *Tatotarho* of the Onondagos; *Togahayon* of the Cayugas;
> *Ganiatario* and *Satagaruyes*, from the two towns of the Senecas,
> &c.… All these names are forever to be kept in remembrance,
> by naming a person in each nation after them…

...They then gave themselves the name *Aquanoshioni*, which means *one house, one family*, and consisted of the Mohawks, Oneidas, Onondagoes, Cayugas, and Senecas. This alliance having been first proposed by a Mohawk chief, the Mohawks rank in the family as the *eldest brother*, the Oneidas as the *eldest son*, the Senecas who were the last at that time had consented to the alliance, were called the *youngest son*; but the Tuscaroras, who joined the confederacy probably one hundred years afterwards, assumed the name, and the Senecas ranked in precedence before them, as being the *next youngest son*, or as we would say, the youngest son but one.[39]

There was considerable debate by 19th century scholars about which "white people" these old traditions were actually referring to, resulting in a range of confederation dates from the mid-1400's to the late 1500's.[40] With the jury still out on that question, the next generation of scholars looked to the heavens for some other way to determine the magical date.

A century of discussion on this issue has centered on a solar eclipse that is said to have occurred when the Senecas were considering whether to accept the Great Law. William Canfield first wrote about it in *Legends of the Iroquois, Told by "The Cornplanter"* (1902), suggesting 1451 as the year of an eclipse, based on a Seneca tradition attributed to Blacksnake, the nephew of Cornplanter. The eclipse occurred when the Senecas and Mohawks were about to annihilate each other. This happened "...when the corn was receiving its last tilling."[41]

Canfield claimed that he found the story in the notes of a surveyor for the Holland Land Company, who was said to have interviewed Cornplanter and Blacksnake on the Allegany Reservation in 1800. He acquired the surveyor's notes and took them back to Allegany to "rework" them with the descendents of Cornplanter and Blacksnake. William Fenton expressed his doubts about Canfield's source in 1998: "This is all quite plausible except that Canfield nowhere identified the original recorder, nor have I succeeded in locating the notebooks, if they even exist."[42]

The second mention of an eclipse appears in "The Return of Hiawatha" (1948) by Paul A. W. Wallace. Wallace's source was Ray Fadden, who got the story from a Tuscarora, George Nash, or *To-re-wa-wa-guhn*:

> When the peace messenger of Deganawidah went to the Seneca Nation he was not at first welcomed, that is, he was not welcomed by one section of the Senecas, that section who dwelt farthest to the west. As they were thinking it over there occurred a strange event. The sun went out and for a little while it was complete darkness. This decided those Senecas who were in doubt. They thought this is a sign that they should join the Confederacy. This happened when the grass was knee high, I think, or when the corn was getting ripe.[43]

These eclipse traditions inspired generations of scholars to turn to astronomy to answer the question of when confederation took place. Wallace, like Canfield before him, proposed the year 1451 for this celestial event. In "Dating the Emergence of the League of the Iroquois" (1991), archaeologist Dean Snow suggested 1536, corresponding with a solar eclipse from that year, and not far—off the mark of establishment scholars, who favored a mid-16th century confederation date.[44] In 1997, Barbara A. Mann and Jerry L. Fields came up with the date of August 31, 1142, publishing their results under the title "A Sign in the Sky: Dating the League of the Haudenosaunee."[45]

Using modern astronomical data, Mann and Fields found a solar eclipse passing through Seneca country on August 31, 1142. This, they say, is when grass is knee high and corn is ripe. (William Fenton rained on this parade by pointing out that these two horticultural references don't actually correlate.[46]) Next, they cite Mohawk Chief Jake Swamp, who asserted that, as of 1994, there have been 145 men who held the title of *Atotárho* since the confederacy was founded. They estimate how long that may have been based the average tenures of popes, kings, and other European officials with life appointments. The two dates match up. Would we have ever heard about it if they didn't?

While I admire the enthusiasm of their scholarship, I remain unconvinced by their argument, based as it is on such peculiar foundations. For instance, the solar eclipse isn't mentioned in the more detailed versions of the confederation story, but is found only in these two obscure sources. The first of these has a dubious provenance, and the second sounds suspiciously like the first with its reference to the height of corn. (Fenton dared to suggest that Nash may have actually *read* Canfield!)

One place where you do find eclipses is in *The Jesuit Relations*. The Jesuits were not above using predictable celestial events to further their work, as we see from an account of a missionary among the Huron:

> We had predicted the Eclipse of the 30th of January, 1646, which began there an hour and a quarter before midnight; our Christians stood expecting it, and suddenly, when it appeared, one of the most fervent, thinking to exercise in this his zeal, awoke some who were sleeping, by saying to them: "Come and see how truthful are our preachers; and strengthen yourselves, by this argument, in the belief of the truths which they preach to us."[47]

The Jesuits employed this tactic among the Oneidas in 1674.[48] Could stories like this have influenced the league tradition that George Nash came to know?

The calculations of Mann and Fields are further undermined by the words of the late Leon Shenandoah, who held the title of Atotárho. In contrast to Jake Swamp's claim that there have been 145 men who held that title since the league's founding, Shenandoah told writer Steve Wall, "It's talked in the Longhouse that there have been over 50 in the last one thousand years."[49] For that matter, there is also no reason to believe that an Onondaga titleholder would have the same life expectancy of a pope or king in Europe.

Mann and Fields admit that there really isn't any agreement among traditional Iroquois as to when the confederacy was founded. Some say it occurred a little bit before European contact, while others say it happened a thousand years ago, two thousand years ago, and even three thousand years ago. So why go to such great lengths to "prove" a specific vintage for the league? And why ignore the fact that it was our own ancestors who first claimed that the Five Nations came together in the generations before Europeans arrived?

The developments cited by archaeologists to suggest a much more recent founding date—such as village "nucleation," palisade construction, and a proliferation of shared pottery styles—really don't need corroboration by alleged celestial signs.[50] Something happened which allowed our people to develop a more sophisticated society, and no other event in our folklore, other than the founding of the Peacemaker's league, corresponds with the "renaissance" that occurred in the Mohawk Valley and the homelands of the Oneida, Onondaga, Cayuga, and Seneca. At least one archaeologists suggests that the Oneida probably hadn't emerged as a separate "nation" as far back in time as the 12th century confederation date proposed by Mann and Fields.[51]

It has been suggested that there are clues to the founding date in the actual league traditions, and I tend to agree with that, especially if you look at as many versions as you can get your hands on. By doing that you will see the story evolving over time, not only getting more complex, but with major changes of plot and character that swirl about until a definite attempt is made to "lock it down" in the late 19th century. Contrast this with the creation story, as recounted by many of the same informants in the same range of time. The different versions seem much more consistent in plot and character, which at first seems puzzling when one considers that the events of the story supposedly happened long before confederation, at the dawn of time. If the confederation epic is recounting a more recent event, one would expect to find more consistency in its details. Instead it is embryonic. This suggests to me that it isn't as old as the creation story, which as you will recall from an earlier chapter, we shared with other Iroquoians like the Huron, and which had ample time to "solidify" in the minds of the people, say for a thousand years.

When viewed as a manifestation of the living culture, which evolves with a people, we can see that the confederation epic was probably based on real events, but over time has accumulated a number of supernatural elements borrowed from both the Iroquoian cultural world (particularly our creation story) and the traditions of other nations. Unlike a typical historical event, the memory of which fades over time, the confederation epic gets more sophisticated as years go by, until it is as fully developed as the creation story, and just as mythic. *How* this happened is much more intriguing than *when* it happened.

9

THAYENDANEGEA ON CONFEDERATION

In addition to being a noted Mohawk leader, *Thayendanegea*, or Joseph Brant, was a history buff. One of his dreams was to write a history of the Iroquois Confederacy. Scholars assumed that Brant never got around to writing his history, focusing instead on translating Holy Scripture into Mohawk, while entrusting his capable protégé, *Teyoninhogarawen*, also known as Major John Norton, with his wealth of knowledge on Iroquoian history.

It turns out that Brant *did* write a history, which we find in the form of an 1801 letter that he wrote to a New York City clergyman, Samuel Miller, in response to a list of questions Miller posed to him. We don't have the actual questions, but we can deduce from the answers that they were about the confederation of the Five Nations.

1. We can say [no] farther respecting the date than that it appears by the transaction to have been a considerable time before the arrival of the Europeans.

2. At the Lower end of the German flats above the Little Falls on Mohawk River — at that place there was a Village of that Nation, situate[d] East and West, the Older Brother named Takanawtagh, had his station at the East gate, he was of a

peaceable disposition, the younger brother named Adegaghtha
was at the West gate and evil [in] declined, he had no peace for
any that came within his reach—these were the two chiefs of
that Village—the Elder brother being grieved at the cruel disposition of the younger, resolved to go westerly and look for
people, and form an alliance with them, he consequently went
and met Odadseghte of the Onidas, by their conversation the
Mohawk was found to be the elder, and therefore the Onida
stiled him father, the Mohawk chief promised to come back
this next day meaning the ensuing year and proceeded farther
on the business of the confederacy—The next year he went to
the Onidas according to the promise, he explained his inten-
tions naming the nine divisions forming the Mohawk
nation—it consisting of three tribes the Wolf, turtle and bear,
and again were each divided into three subdivisions—the
[Mohawk] *Onid* got up and sung, mentioning that his [son]
father and him were united and that his [son] *father* would be
the superior upon this [the Onida] *Mohawk* stopped him, [then
the Mohawk] and rose, express[ed]ing by a song that *it should
not be so but* that they both should be equal [at this the Onidas
were satisfied]—Upon this being passed the Onida wished to
stop him [to rest a little] saying he would throw a tree in the
way that he could not get over upon this the other stiled him
the big tree and they are yet so called. They went together to
Onondaga, they found the chief there very obstinate, they
with difficulty brought him to agree the Mohawk stiling him
brother, and equal in the confederacy[;] when they went to
return home, one of the young men had forgot his maukissins
and went back to look for them, as he was by the side of the
house he heard the Onondaga singing that what the Father
and son had proposed to him did not suit him and that he
could not wear it—when he overtook them he told what
he had heard—in consequence of which they agreed to
return next year—they did and the Mohawk then proposed
to the Onondaga, that he should keep the Council fire of
the confederacy, and the he should carry their title—these

condescensions brought him to agree—and they proceeded to Cayuga their chief had a big pipe, for which reason they give the nation that name [Shononenaweandwane], they stiled him their son, and brother to the Onidas—From there they went on to the Senecas, there was two principal chiefs of these, Kanyadariyoh and Shadekaroinyis, they also agreed to the confederacy[;] in consequence of their frontier situation they called them roninhohhont—or the doorkeeper.

3. The names of those were Tekanawaidagh of the Mohawk, Otatsighte, Onida, Thadodarhoagh Onondaga— Shonónawendówane Cayuga, Kanyataríyoh & Shadekaroínyis of the Senecas [;] this chief's name was Thadodarhonagh for that reason he is yet called roghseanakighte.

4. The conditions of the confederacy seem to be expressed by the titles given each other as that of brothers and sons, representing that brotherly and filial love which was to guide their conduct to each other—this was further cemented by friendships between individuals of the several nations which was held very sacred[;] in consequence of this they considered themselves as mutually bound to partake in each others good or bad success.

5. The space of time from the Mohawks, and Onidas meeting until the Cayugas joined the confederacy was about four years, the Senecas joined [it] *the confederacy* some time after

6. The have no tradition of having dwelt at any other place than the Mohawk river, the first mentioned is at the Hill called Anthony's nose, where the village was under the Hill, which by an earthquake fell on it and destroyed it[52]

Brant's version has *Tekanawtagh* and his wicked brother *Adergaghtha* as chiefs of a Mohawk village, whereas later versions say the former was from the Bay of Quinte are north of Lake Ontario, and the latter was from Onondaga—assuming, of course, that Adergaghtha is just a garbled version of Aionwà:tha. It's also devoid of the shape-shifting messengers, the magical canoe, and the snakes in *Thadodarhoagh's* hair that figure prominently in later accounts. Brant may have downplayed these supernatural elements for his audience, a New York clergyman, because he may have wanted to impress upon him that confederation was a real, historic event, but there is also the possibility that these elements weren't yet a part of the league tradition—or at the very least, the league tradition that the Iroquois let outsiders know about.

In 1815, Ephraim Williams, a Rev War veteran and a trader among the Onondaga since 1784, was also given a "stripped-down" account of confederation, as cited in William Dunlop's *History of New Netherlands, Province and State of New York* (1839).

An inferior chief of the Onondagas conceived the bright idea of union and of a great council of the chiefs of the Five Nations. The principal chief opposed it. He was a great warrior and feared to lose his influence as a head man of the Onondagas. This was a selfish man. The younger chief, whom we all call Owego, was silenced; but he determined in secret to attempt the great political work. This was a man who loved the welfare of others. To make long journeys and be absent for several days while hunting, would cause suspicion, because it was common. He left home as if to hunt; but taking a circuitous path through the woods, for all this great country was then a wilderness, he made his way to the village or castle of the Mohawks. He consulted some of the leaders of that tribe, and they received the scheme favorably; he visited the Oneidas, and gained the assent of their chief; he then returned home. After a time he made another hunt; and another; thus, by degrees, visiting the Cayugas and Senecas, and gained the assent of all to a great council to be held at Onondaga. With consummate art he then gained over his chief, by convincing him of the advantages of the confederacy, and agreeing that he should be considered author of the plan. The great council met, and the chief of the Onondagas made use of the figurative argument, taught him by Owego, which was the same that we read of in the fable, where a father teaches his sons the value of union by taking one stick from a bundle, and showing how feeble it was and easily broken, and when bound together the bundle resisted his utmost strength.[53]

It is probably safe to assume that the more fantastic elements of the story were held back in both of these cases. We know this because Joseph Brant's protégé, Major John Norton, recorded another confederation account in his 1816 journal which goes into considerable detail about such matters.

10

TEYONINHOGARAWEN'S LEAGUE TRADITION

Major John Norton, or *Teyoninhogarawen*, was the son of Cherokee and Scottish parents. He eventually wrote the book that Joseph Brant dreamed of writing, and sent it to Europe in search of a publisher. Financing for the endeavor never materialized, and the manuscript gathered dust in the archives of Alnwick Castle in Northumberland, England, for more than a century. Scholars eventually rediscovered and published the manuscript in 1970. It was well worth the wait. *The Journal of Major John Norton, 1816,* is a treasure trove of early Iroquois history and lore.[54]

Norton presents two versions of the creation story and an Onondaga confederation epic that is rife with fantastic elements, such as snakes in the sorcerer's hair and messengers who change into birds. This version gives an Onondaga identity to *Hayouwaghtengh* (Aionwà:tha) but still identifies *Tekanawitigh* (Tekanawí:ta) as a Mohawk chief. There is no mention of a mystical canoe of any kind, stone or otherwise.

A notable feature of this version is that it begins with a migration story that echoes Lafitau's "Gaihonariosk" scenario. Prominence is given to an ancient matriarch who "commands" the people:

> The Onondagas relate, "that, before they had collected at Onondague, there was a very extensive village up Salmon Creek, a River about eighteen miles to the Eastward of Oswego. That there a difference arose between some of the principal people, and they agreed to remove and separate.

When they were all embarked in their canoes, one of their oldest and most respected women addressed them thus.

'My Grandchildren, why should you be burdened any longer with me, now worn out with years? You are going to wander in search of a settlement, I shall only incumber you, and be distressed myself in being taken from my native place, and in beholding you separate. I command you therefore to lay me between the parting canoes, that when you separate, I may be let fall into the pure and transparent waters of the Lake.'

In obedience to this request, they ranged in a line the canoes of each party, that were to pursue separate routes. The two leading canoes approached each other; the old woman was laid on a bier between them; they parted, and she fell into the water, which was clear, transparent and deep. They followed her with their eyes, and as soon as the movement of the water had subsided, instead of seeing their Grandmother any more, they saw a large sturgeon. They then parted, one division pursued the route towards Cataraqui, and before they had got out of hearing of each other, they had begun to speak a different language. From these, they say, have sprung the Nations of the Algonquin or Chippawa language, which the Five Nations call Dewakanka. The other party took a western course, till arriving at a Creek, (still called Ondatshaigh, from the circumstance of disputing there) about nine miles west of Oswego; some were inclined to ascend it, and others to continue westerly along the shore of the Lake. This difference of inclination caused a dispute, and they separated, each following the bent of their inclinations: those who went up the Creek were headed by a Chief called Hayouwaghtengh.

After ascending a few miles, they encamped: – some went to hunt, others to fish. Those who had been engaged in the Chace returned in the evening with an account of a fine stream, that ran a different course, being not many miles distant. It was determined to move there. They came there and fixed their habitations, finding salmon in abundance, and good hunting.

Some time after, the Salmon ceasing to pass, Hayouwaghtengh then sent two men up the stream to learn the cause of this change. They came to a village, and were conducted to the house of the Chief, who asked them from whence they had come? They said, 'Hayouwaghtengh our Chief has sent us to see what had stopped the fish from coming down the River ', the Chief replied, 'You see it is the weirs we have made to catch them; but as your people suffer from it, you had better throw down the stones, we have raised, and let the fish pass. You may then return, and tell your Chief, that we invite him, and his people to come, and be our neighbours; you can settle on the opposite side of the river, we will then jointly rebuild the weir, and the half on the other side of the river shall be your property.' The men hesitated to pull down the weir, until the people of the village began to demolish it themselves.

Having returned, they informed Hayouwaghtengh what they had seen, and of the invitation sent to him — from the Chief of the village. The fish had now come down the Stream since the demolition of the Weirs, yielding them abundance of food. They made preparations to move, and to accept of the friendly invitation. Arriving there, the Chief and people of the village received them with open arms, helping them to build their huts, and then they jointly refilled the Weirs.

After they had lived here some time, they sent men to view the country down the River, who, descending, came to the outlet of the Onondaga Lake, and met there some people from the Village at the Oswego Falls, who had come on the same errand. They were surprised at the sulphureous smell proceeding from these waters, and unable to account for the cause they call it Otaghtonghserou which implies. — The *Place of Dread.*

They proceeded into the Lake, and finding the waters of it brackish, they passed by the Great Salt Spring, some of which they found incrusted on the ground, the Sun having evaporated its humidity. They tasted it, and were gratified by the novelty of its flavour. They saw the lofty hill of Onondague, covered with its forests of oak, rising above the rest, and the smoke of Thatotarho's fire (the Chief of the village) ascending to the Clouds. Both parties returned to their respective Villages, and it was there agreed to assemble at Onondague...[55]

At this point in the narrative, tragedy enters the life of Aionwà:tha, a theme that recurs in later accounts.

...Hayouwaghtengh had three beautiful granddaughters; — a man of the name of Oghsinou desired to have the oldest, but she refused him. He is said to have possessed supernatural powers, and having transformed himself every night into an Owl, perched on a tree near the house, and intermixed with the notes of his new assumed species, dreadful to children, human speech, repeating. 'The Granddaughter of Hayouwaghtengh must admit the embraces of Oghsinou.' In the day time, he repeated his addresses and entreaties; but notwithstanding these or his nocturnal visits, in a borrowed form, and mysterious commands, the lovely Maid persisted in refusing him. She was seized with sickness and died. Oghsinou continuing his visits, armed with Owlish dread, afflicting with the same notes, the disconsolate family, Hayouwaghtengh seized his bow and quiver, and going under the tree whence issued the disconsolate notes of the ill omened bird of night, he took aim, and down it came tumbling, resuming the natural form of Oghsinou as he expired.

They arrived at Onondague and met there the people of the village of Oghswego-Falls, who were of the Bear Tribe; they were also rejoined by those who had parted with them at Ondatshaigh. They awaited the arrival of the Wolf Tribe, — at last they made their appearance crossing the Lake in Canoes. Thatotarho sate on the Hill Side: he saw them approach on the Lake; his mind was seized with a malevolent fit; he raised a blast, exclaiming, 'these dilatory people, do they appear at last?' Their canoes disappeared as if swallowed up by the waves. However, the Wolf Tribe was again heard of. As they advanced, it was proposed to meet in a sequestered part of the woods. They *met* there; but the power of Thatotarho yet followed them, and caused a high soaring Eagle to fall; — it happened to reach the ground at the feet of the Granddaughter of Hayouwaghtengh, who was far gone in pregnancy. The youth who crowded there to obtain the choice feathers, hurt her, that she died.

This loss so affected Hayouwaghtengh, that he rejected all comfort and nourishment: he laid himself down in his Cabin; the principal people assembled there, but he could not look upon them. After some days, he began to sing; they listened, caught the air & joined in the chorus; the burden of the song was, 'I am about to leave you; for the solace of my old age has been taken from me!'[56]

As the faithkeeper of a far away tribe once said, "a prophet receives no honor in his own country."[57] If Aionwà:tha had a message to share, he would find his audience elsewhere—and so he leaves Onondaga and begins his journey southward.

When he had ended his song, he took up his pouch, and bid them farewell, recommending his niece to fill his place: he rejected all their repeated entreaties to remain, — and proceeded on a Southern course, he came to one of the branches of the Susquehannok called Atchineankigh, and soon discovered the abodes of men: he approached them, and the people saluted him by name. The Chief calling him into his house, said, 'Remain with us; you shall have a voice in all our Councils, I will divide with you the authority of Chief.' He accepted this invitation; (which indeed was given by people of the same dialect) and remained with them a little while; but perceiving that they did not shew him that respect which they had promised in their invitation, he took up his pouch, and proceeded down the stream, until he came to another village; there entering the first house, he sate down on a birth by the fire-side. The woman of the house re-entering, and seeing a venerable old man of lofty stature seated by the fire, she ran to the house of the nearest Chief, to tell him that such a Man was there.

'It is Hayouwaghtengh,' he exclaimed, rising up and going to him. On entering the house, he saluted him, and took him by the hand, saying, 'come to my house, there is a birth for you.' They went out together and leading him into his house, he shewed him his birth; they had hardly seated themselves, when a young man came, saying, 'I am sent by your brother to call Hayouwaghtengh to his house.' 'Yes,' replied the other, 'that is always the way, when anyone comes here. Tell him to come to us first.' He then said to Hayouwaghtengh, 'when he arrives, I shall take him out of doors, and amuse him a little; in the mean time, you must cut his bow string, almost through, leaving only a sufficiency to hold it together until pulled.'

The brother came; the Chief took him out, and leaving his bow in the house, Hayouwaghtengh cut the string as directed. They then re-entered, and it was proposed to go to the Brother's house. When they had gone a little way, the wicked brother aimed an arrow at Hayouwaghtengh; but in bending the bow, the string broke, and the arrow fell harmless at his feet. 'Ah! ' exclaimed the Chief['s] brother, 'this is the way, that my brother always serves me.' And the other said, 'You are fortunate that my string broke, or I certainly should have felled you to the ground.'

They now seemed to forget all, and were great friends: both brothers requested him to stay with them, saying that he should have an equal voice in their councils and an equal authority with themselves. But, in a little time, Hayouwaghtengh saw them go to Council without calling him; neither was he consulted on any affair; therefore taking up his pouch, he crossed Atchineankegh, and following the course of the stream, he came to the confluence of another branch, (which I think is called Oghquaga), there seeing no traces of men, he thought that he had passed the bounds of their habitations; he did not cross this stream, but ascending along its banks, near its source he came to a pond or small Lake, where he saw geese shedding their feathers, and assuming human shapes: some had almost acquired the complete form; he called out to them, 'who or what are you, that presume to take the form of man?' They then arose and flew off. He passed through the Lake, which was now dried, and on the slime which covered its bottom, he discovered some wampum which he collected and put in his pouch...[58]

This is the first mention of Aionwà:tha's discovery of wampum in the literature. Inspired by his grief, the ritual use of wampum in the condolence ceremony would become a defining feature of Iroquois diplomacy.

The narrative continues with Aionwà:tha entering Mohawk territory, where he is welcomed by a chief, Tekanawí:ta, given here as *Tekannawitagh:*

...A little farther on, he got on the head stream of Scohari, which he descended until he came to its confluence with the Mohawk River, where there stood at that time a Village of the Mohawks or Kanyenkega. He entered a house, and seated himself on the birth. After a while, the woman entered, he had then strung the wampum and holding it in his hand, was repeating a speech. The woman immediately ran out, and telling the Chief, that there was a man of remarkable appearance, who had come to her house; he said, 'it is

Hayouwaghtengh that has arrived at our Village, — bring him here.'

Hayouwaghtengh entered; — the Chief (whose name was Tekannawitagh,) pointed to a birth on the opposite side of the fire, saying, 'that place is yours; we shall have the same house; and you shall have an equal voice in our Council. What has happened to you, and constrained you to leave your family, your friends, and your country?' 'Thatotarho' (answered Hayouwaghtengh) 'is angry.'

Tekanawitagh thereupon called a meeting of the Mohawks, whom when they had assembled, he addressed thus: — 'Who is there among you that will go and search out the habitation of Thatotarho?' Two young men offered to go; they assumed the form of cranes and flew over without observing the intermediate villages, until they had reached the Genesee: there, having found pleasant plains, they never returned; establishing themselves among the Ondowaga, of which Nation their descendants now form a Clan or Tribe.

After they had lost patience in waiting for their return, another meeting was called: some of the Warriors then observed, that it was useless to wait for these people any longer, for having found some pleasant prairie productive of ground beans, they had remained there contented and happy, unconcerned about them, having found all they wanted. This was said, referring to the nature of cranes, who are very fond of these kind of beans, and whose form the messengers had assumed.

Two other men were sent, who assuming the appearance of ravens, flew until they saw smoke rising, then descending they resumed their human form, and approaching the Village, they were met by people who having saluted them, conducted them to the house of the Chief, who addressed them thus: 'Where have you come from; and to what place are you now directing your course?' They replied, 'We are in search of the habitation of Thatotarho who (it is said) is angry. Can you tell us where he dwells?' The Chief answered, 'we hear that his abode is on the side of yonder mountain, and sometimes we see the smoke ascending to the clouds from thence. When you return, we will throw a tree in the path' (implying by this an invitation *for* them to turn off it to their Village, which is called Oniada.) They continued their route, with the aid of the wings of the raven, until they came within sight of the Village, when they descended, and resumed their proper shapes; then proceeding on the side of the hill, within view of the habitation, they met a person of whom they enquired *for* the abode of Thatotarho: he replied, 'Speak softly, that is the house in which he dwells.' They went in and saw him seated; he was a person of a frightful deformed aspect, with hissing serpents hanging from his head instead of hair.

In returning through the country of the Oniadas, they informed them, that they had found out Thatotarho, astonishing them with the dreadful account which they gave of his appearance. They arrived safe at the Mohawk Village, and as soon as they had given a narrative of the discovery which they had made, Tekanawitigh made preparations *for* undertaking his intended embassy. Tekanawitagh laid down the wampum he appropriated for the occasion: another Chief laying down his proportion said, 'Sadekariwategh, wakerighwaghsondere,' that is, 'an equal affair I add.' Hayouwaghtengh then said, 'tekarigkhogea wakerighwageron, — I put mine among the whole affair.' The first was called from this expression, Satekariwategh, the other Tekarighhogea.

These are of course some of the title names of Mohawk chiefs that are carried down into modern times, given in their original context. New chiefs are given these names to keep the story (and its message) current and fresh in the minds of each new generation.

Tekanawitagh set off for Onondagui and ascending the rapid stream of the Mohawk River, he came to

Tehikaghkwetsni, now called Utica: there he met an Onida, with a wolf skin quiver. The Onida saluted him by the title of brother, cousin and friend; — to all of which Tekanawitagh made no reply. He then said, 'I salute you my father;' — true my son (returned Tekanawitagh,) 'for none of the trees of the forest are equal to me in age: the willows of the River's banks alone approach it.' He then continued, 'where are you going my father?' he replied, 'I am going to soothe the angry feelings of Thatotarho; to reform his rugged appearance, and endeavour to make him like other men.' He then named the Onida, Odatsheghte, or the Quiver Carrier, who replied. — 'Father, the day is now too far spent; let us remain at home this night. In the morning, if you will return, I shall throw a tree across the path to detain you a little while, and then we shall proceed together to the place where the smoke of Thatotarho's fires arise.' This was spoken allegorically to the season.

Tekanawitagh returned home, and in the spring got ready for his embassy. They came to the abode of Odatsheghte, who entertained him kindly. The people of the Village assembled together, Odatsheghte rose and sung, 'This is my father; he is my superior, and I will follow him.' Tekanawitagh interrupting him said, 'that will not do, you must sing.' 'My father and I shall risk together; — we are the same,' Odatsheghte immediately complied, which satisfied him.

They went on to Onondague where they arrived, and entered the abode of Thatotarho. He was seated at the further end of the house, without any clothing to cover the deformities of his body, his hair was frightful serpents. Tekanawitagh and the other Chiefs approached him, they spoke, delivering wampum until they had removed all his deformities: they then covered his body with a garment and put mocasins on his feet. After they thought, that

they had restored him to his natural state, and removed
every deformity, — they returned towards home. On the
road, one of the young men having forgot his moccasins
which he had hung up on the out side of the house,
ran back for them; and when he came to take them off,
he heard Thatotarho inside, singing: the burden of
the song was, 'What these men have put on me, does not
fit me.'

Many have suggested that the "frightful serpents" in *Thatotarho's* hair
were simply a metaphor for mental illness, but they may have a more
mundane explanation. Strips of snake skin may have been incorporated
in the man's headgear, perhaps as a token of some form of medicine
society to which he belonged. For all we know, he may have had real
snakes nesting in his hair. (Greeks probably have this same discussion
about Medusa.)

He then followed the party; when he came up with the Chiefs,
he told them of the song Thatotarho was singing. Then
Tekanawitagh said, 'next year we shall return, and try if we
cannot satisfy him.' He named the Oniadas, Harontakowa,
besides the ancient name of Oniyout, which they took from
their situation, this latter implying — A *standing stone* — the
former — *Big Tree.*

He agreed with Odatseghte, the principal Chief of this
place, to revisit Thatotarho the following year, to make him
the Keeper of the Council Fire of the confederacy, which was
to be placed at his Village, as another expedient to retain him
firmly attached to the league. He then continued till he
reached home where he made his people acquainted with the
result of his embassy.

Next summer he again set out, taking his son Odatsheghte
by the hand as he passed his Village. They came to the abode
of Thatotarho, who now made a more comely appearance than
he did at the former meeting: he seemed to improve under

their hands. The task which yet remained for them to perform was to rectify the concealed parts, to interest his heart in the welfare of the confederacy by inducing him to think, that his own interest and honour was linked to that of the public, to insinuate by this means into his mind, the seeds of brotherly love and affection.

Tekanawitagh and his son Odatseghte now informed Thatotarho, that they had come to a resolution to appoint him the Guardian or Keeper of the Council Fire of the Confederacy; that *they left their minds with him.* In consideration of this station, they gave him the name of Roghseanakighte — (Title Bearer). They presented him with a wing wherewith to keep the Council Fire-place clean, and a staff wherewith to cast away any worm, snake or venomous creature that might approach it; (implying whatever might interrupt the tranquillity of the Confederacy;) but should it be of too great weight for him alone to remove it, he was desired to shout, and the whole of the Confederacy would assemble to render him assistance.

This mark of respect, so far pleased Thatotarho, that there is no more said of his being refractory. Not long after the commencement, the Cayugas acceded to the Confederacy; they were received into it as a son, and younger brother to the Oniada or Oniyout, — and as such received the name of Shonnounaweantowa or Great Pipe. After them the Ondowaga were added as a younger brother to the Mohawks and Onondagas, and as such received the title of Ronninhohhonte, implying The Supporter of the Gate or Door on which the Gate is hung." In this tradition, there is also some variety in the manner it is related by the different

Nations; but all concur in substance: And whether they were induced to form this Confederacy, the more effectually to defend themselves, or to carry on hostillities against some neighbouring nations, no traditions remain to inform us.[59]

We can take pride in the fact that of all great legends throughout the world, ours is probably the only one that ends not with the destruction of the villain, but with his healing and recovery. It teaches us that anyone can have a change of heart, including those we consider the most evil.

Teyoninhogarawen's account of confederation marks the beginning of a new genre in the Iroquoian literature—the *league tradition*. This "living history" would evolve over time, as all living things do, but it would never change so much that the people who gave it life—and kept it alive—would cease to recognize it.

11

AIONWÀ:THA AND THE BEAUTIFUL TALISMANIC CANOE

Once upon a time I shared a vendor's booth at the Foxwood Casino's powwow with Tom Huff, the noted Seneca stone carver. He gave me a piece of soapstone to carve when things got slow with my T-shirt sales. Since retired white people in Connecticut don't wear T-shirts that say things like *Columbus Day Sucks*, I had plenty of time to carve myself a tiny stone canoe.

I asked Tom if he thought it was possible for someone to carve a canoe out of stone, as the Peacemaker is said to have done, and if it would float. He said, "Sure, it's possible. They make giant aircraft carriers out of steel, don't they? It's all about displacement." Having said that, he took my little stone canoe and began to carve away at it until you could practically see light through the stone. Then he popped the lid off my coffee cup and placed the canoe on the surface of the coffee. *And wouldn't you know it, it sank like a rock!*

That being said, I still believe it is possible that someone could carve a stone canoe, and when this book hits the bestseller list, I will buy a big chunk of stone and hire Tom Huff to carve one.

The question of whether anyone actually *did* carve a stone canoe won't be resolved quite so easily, as it doesn't begin to emerge in the literature until the late 1800's.

Henry B. Schoolcraft's *Information Respecting the History, Condition and Prospects of the Indian Tribes of the United States* (1853) contains an

Onondaga league tradition attributed to *De-hat-ka-tons*, or Abraham La Fort, that describes a "canoe which would move without paddles," but there is no mention of it being made of stone.

HIAWATHA, OR, THE ORIGIN OF THE ONONDAGA COUNCIL-FIRE.

TARENYAWAGO taught the Six Nations arts and knowledge. He had a canoe which would move without paddles. It was only necessary to will it, to compel it to go. With this he ascended the streams and lakes. He taught the people to raise corn and beans, removed obstructions from their watercourses, and made their fishing-grounds clear. He helped them to get the mastery over the great monsters which overran the country, and thus prepared the forests for their hunters. His wisdom was as great as his power. The people listened to him with admiration, and followed his advice gladly. There was nothing in which he did not excel good hunters, brave warriors, and eloquent orators.

He gave them wise instructions for observing the laws and maxims of the Great Spirit. Having done these things, he laid aside the high powers of his public mission, and resolved to set them an example of how they should live.

For this purpose, he selected a beautiful spot on the southern shore of one of the lesser and minuter lakes, which is called Tioto (Cross lake) by the natives, to this day. Here he erected his lodge, planted his field of corn, kept by him his magic canoe, and selected a wife. In relinquishing his former position, as a subordinate power to the Great Spirit, he also dropped his name, and, according to his present situation, took that of Hiawatha, meaning a person of very great wisdom, which the people spontaneously bestowed on him.

He now lived in a degree of respect scarcely inferior to that which he before possessed. His words and counsels were implicitly obeyed. The people flocked to him from all quarters, for advice and instruction. Such persons as had been prominent in following his precepts, he favored, and they became eminent on the war-path and in the council-room.

When Hiawatha assumed the duties of an individual, at Tioto, he carefully drew out from the water his beautiful talismanic canoe, which had served for horses and chariot, in his initial excursions through the Iroquois territories, and it was carefully secured on land, and never used except in his journeys to attend the general councils. He had elected to become a member of the Onondaga tribe, and chose the residence of this people, in the shady recesses of their fruitful valley, as the central point of their government.

After the termination of his higher mission from above, years passed away in prosperity, and the Onondagas assumed an elevated rank, for their wisdom and learning, among the other tribes, and there was not one of these which did not yield its assent to their high privilege of lighting the general council-fire.[60]

This tradition not only gives Aionwà:tha a mystical canoe, but identifies himself as a manifestation of *Tarenyawago*—undoubtedly the being we know as Teharonhiawá:kon, the "good twin" of the creation story. It also confirms the notion that an outside threat forced the Five Nations to confederate:

Suddenly there arose a great alarm at the invasion of a ferocious band of warriors from the north of the Great Lakes. As they advanced, an indiscriminate slaughter was made of men, women, and children. Destruction threatened to be alike the fate of those who boldly resisted, or quietly submitted. The public alarm was extreme. Hiawatha advised them not to waste their efforts in a desultory manner, but to call a general council of all the tribes that could be gathered together from the east to the west; and he appointed the meeting to take place on an eminence on the banks of Onondaga lake.

Accordingly all the chief men assembled at this spot. The occasion brought together vast multitudes of men, women, and children; for there was an expectation of some great deliverance. Three days had already elapsed, and there began to be a general anxiety lest Hiawatha should not arrive. Messengers were despatched for him to Tioto, who found him in a pensive mood, to whom he communicated his strong presentiments that evil betided his attendance. These were overruled by the strong representations of the messengers, and he again put his wonderful vessel in its element, and set out for the council, taking his only daughter with him. She timidly took her seat in the stern, with a light paddle, to give direction to the vessel; for the strength of the current of the Seneca river was sufficient to give velocity to the motion till arriving at So-hah-hi, the Onondaga outlet. At this point the powerful exertions of the aged chief were required, till they entered on the bright bosom of the Onondaga.[61]

In later chapters of this history we will see how this "beautiful talismanic canoe" that didn't require paddles evolved into a white stone canoe. Before we get to that, however, we will continue with the rest of the La Fort/Schoolcraft narrative, because it picks up on a much darker theme first mentioned by Major John Norton: the tragic fate of Aionwà:tha's female offspring.

The grand council, that was to avert the threatened danger, was quickly in sight, and sent up its shouts of welcome, as the venerated man approached, and landed in front of the assemblage. An ascent led up the banks of the lake to the place occupied by the council. As he walked up this, a loud sound was heard in the air above, as if caused by some rushing current of wind. Instantly the eyes of all were directed upward to the sky, where a spot of matter was discovered descending rapidly, and every instant enlarging in its size and velocity. Terror and alarm were the first impulses, for it appeared to be descending into their midst, and they scattered in confusion.

Hiawatha, as soon as he had gained the eminence, stood still, and caused his daughter to do the same; deeming it cowardly to fly, and impossible, if it were attempted, to divert the designs of the Great Spirit. The descending object had now assumed a more definite aspect, and as it came down, revealed the shape of a gigantic white bird, with wide extended and pointed wings, which came down, swifter and swifter, with a mighty swoop, and crushed the girl to the earth. Not a muscle was moved in the face of Hiawatha. His daughter lay dead before him, but the great and mysterious white bird was also destroyed by the shock. Such had been the violence of the concussion, that it had completely buried its beak and head in the ground. But the most wonderful sight was the carcase of the prostrated bird, which was covered with beautiful plumes of snow-white shining feathers. Each warrior stepped up, and decorated himself with a plume. And it hence became a custom to assume this kind of feathers on the war-path. Succeeding generations substituted the plumes of the white heron, which led this bird to be greatly esteemed.

But yet a greater wonder ensued. On removing the carcase of the bird, not a human trace could be discovered of the daughter. She had completely vanished. At this the father was greatly afflicted in spirits, and disconsolate...[62]

As recounted by Schoolcraft, Abraham La Fort's league tradition mentions the tragic death of Aionwà:tha's daughter, whereas Major John Norton's earlier version says it was his three granddaughters who died. Variations on the theme become a staple of the story; it inspires Aionwà:tha to invent the condolence ceremony in later accounts. It's probably the only part of the story that has any factual basis, the death of a young female being particularly devastating to a matrilineal society. Some accounts even have the young woman dying with a child in her womb.

In this version, Aionwà:tha overcomes his grief and urges the assembled nations to unify:

…But he roused himself, as from a lethargy, and walked to the head of the council with a dignified air, covered with his simple robe of wolfskins; taking his seat with the chief warriors and counsellors, and listening with attentive gravity to the plans of the different speakers. One day was given to these discussions; on the next day, he arose and said:

My friends and brothers; you are members of many tribes, and have come from a great distance. We have met to promote the common interest, and our mutual safety. How shall it be accomplished? To oppose these northern hordes in tribes singly, while we are at variance often with each other, is impossible. By uniting in a common band of brotherhood, we may hope to succeed. Let this be done, and we shall drive the enemy from our land. Listen to me by tribes.

You (the Mohawks), who are sitting under the shadow of the Great Tree, whose roots sink deep in the earth, and whose branches spread wide around, shall be the first nation, because you are warlike and mighty.

You (the Oneidas), who recline your bodies against the Everlasting Stone, that cannot be moved, shall be the second nation, because you always give wise counsel.

You (the Onondagas), who have your habitation at the foot of the Great Hills, and are overshadowed by their crags, shall be the third nation, because you are all greatly gifted in speech.

You (the Senecas), whose dwelling is in the Dark Forest, and whose home is everywhere, shall be the fourth nation, because of your superior cunning in hunting.

And you (the Cayugas), the people who live in the Open Country, and possess much wisdom, shall be the fifth nation, because you understand better the art of raising corn and beans, and making houses.

Unite, you five nations, and have one common interest, and no foe shall disturb and subdue you. You, the people who are as the feeble bushes, and you, who are a fishing people, may place yourselves under our protection, and we will defend you. And you of the south and of the west may do the same, and we will protect you. We earnestly desire the alliance and friendship of you all.

Brothers, if we unite in this great bond, the Great Spirit will smile upon us, and we shall be free, prosperous, and happy. But if we remain as we are, we shall be subject to his frown. We shall be enslaved, ruined, perhaps annihilated. We may perish under the war-storm, and our names be no longer remembered by good men, nor be repeated in the dance and song.

Brothers, these are the words of Hiawatha. I have said it. I am done.

The next day the plan of union was again considered, and adopted by the council. Conceiving this to be the accomplishment of his mission to the Iroquois, the tutelar patron of this rising confederacy addressed them in a speech elaborate with wise counsels, and then announced his withdrawal to the skies. At its conclusion, he went down to the shore, and assumed his seat in his mystical vessel. Sweet music was heard in the air at the same moment, and as its cadence floated in the ears of the wondering multitude, it rose in the air, higher and higher, till it vanished from the sight, and disappeared in the celestial regions inhabited only by Owayneo and his hosts.[63]

Eventually the Iroquois keepers of this tradition took this "mystical vessel" away from Aionwà:tha and gave it to that old Mohawk chief, Tekanawí:ta, and along with it, his mystical connection to the "good son" of the creation story. As we will see, they then relocated Tekanawí:ta to Canada and gave him membership in a new band.

12

EVOLUTION OF A PEACEMAKER

The transformation of Tekanawí:ta in the literature begins after 1883, the year that Horatio Hale published *The Iroquois Book of Rites*. Hale describes Tekanawí:ta as a Mohawk chief with a well-established, if complicated, family tree. As in earlier accounts, Aionwà:tha's tragic loss is the catalyst for his sojourn in the wilderness, which brings him into the domain of Tekanawí:ta, given here as *Dekanawidah*.

Early one morning he arrived at a Canienga town, the residence of the noted chief Dekanawidah, whose name, in point of celebrity, ranks in Iroquois tradition with those of Aionwatha and Atotarho. It is probable that he was known by reputation to Hiawatha, and not unlikely that they were related. According to one account Dekanawidah was an Onondaga, adopted among the Caniengas. Another narrative makes him a Canienga by birth. The probability seems to be that he was the son of an Onondaga father, who had been adopted by the Caniengas, and of a Canienga mother. That he was not of pure Canienga blood is shown by the fact, which is remembered, that his father had had successively three wives, one belonging to each of the three clans, Bear, Wolf, and Tortoise, which composed the Canienga nation. If the father had been of that nation (Canienga), he would have belonged to one of the Canienga clans, and could not then (according to the Indian law) have married into it. He had seven sons, including Dekanawidah, who, with their families, dwelt together in one of the "long houses" common in that day among the Iroquois. These ties of kindred, together with this fraternal strength, and his reputation as a sagacious councillor, gave Dekanawidah great influence among his people. But, in the Indian sense, he was not the leading chief. This position belonged to Tekarihoken (better known in books as Tecarihoga), whose primacy as the first chief of the eldest among the Iroquois nations was then, and is still, universally admitted. Each nation has always had a head-chief, to whom belonged the hereditary right and duty of lighting the council fire and taking the first place in public meetings. But among the Indians, as in other communities, hereditary rank and personal influence do not always, or indeed, ordinarily, go together. If Hiawatha could gain over Dekanawidah to his views, he would have done much toward the accomplishment of his purposes.[64]

When the unification of the Five Nations is complete, Hale has Aionwà:tha adopted by the Mohawks, his name preserved in the list of title names that are handed down from chief to chief, right after the name of Tekarihó:ken. Tekanawí:ta declines a similar honor.

"Let others have successors," he said proudly, "for others can advise you like them. But I am the founder of your league, and nobody else can do what I have done."

The boast was not unwarranted. Though planned by another, the structure had been reared mainly by his labors. But the Five Nations, while yielding abundant honor to the memory of Dekanawidah, have never regarded him with the same affectionate reverence which has always clung to the name of Hiawatha. His tender and lofty wisdom, his wide-reaching benevolence, and his fervent appeals to their better sentiments, enforced by the eloquence of which he was master, touched chords in the popular heart which have continued to respond until this day. Fragments of the speeches in which he addressed the council and the people of the league are still remembered and repeated.[65]

Shortly after Hale wrote those words, they proved prophetic. Tekanawí:ta supplanted Aionwà:tha as the central character in the epic.

This all began in the days of *Da-yo-de-ka-ne*, or Seth Newhouse, the half-Mohawk, half-Onondaga traditionalist of the Six Nations Reserve at Grand River. In 1880 he wrote *Constitution of the Five Nations Indian Confederacy*, followed by *The Cosmogony of De-ka-na-wi-da's Government* in 1885. Like previous versions, Newhouse has Aionwà:tha meeting Tekanawí:ta in the Mohawk Valley, where he is a chief. William Fenton tells us that Newhouse added more material to the manuscript after 1899:

> Having consumed two hundred pages of the ledger, Dayodekane starts over again with what he calls "Chapter II" (pages 200-235). Here we find a repetition of the Dekanawidah legend, but this time in Mohawk and English.... Somewhat earlier (pages 169-173), aware that he had omitted the significant episode Dekanawidah's virgin birth, Dayodekane sought to supply the deficiency and also include a map to illustrate the route of Dekanawidah's travels (page 173).[66]

Newhouse spent years working on the manuscript and consulted elders in both the United States and Canada. It is said that he even made his own ink, so insistent was he that the manuscript be as "Indian" as possible. His efforts to preserve the ancient workings of the confederacy occurred in the era when Canada began to impose elections on our ancestors.

When his manuscript was presented to the chiefs, they rejected it, choosing instead to draft their own version. This was completed in 1900. Duncan Campbell Scott published it in 1912.[67] Seneca ethnologist Arthur C. Parker included it, along with Seth Newhouse's revised account, in "The Constitution of the Five Nations or the Iroquois Book of the Great Law," published in *The New York State Museum Bulletin* of 1916, and later reprinted in *Parker on the Iroquois* in 1967.[68]

Both versions make Tekanawí:ta the focus of the epic, whereas earlier versions emphasized Aionwà:tha. Of the two, the chiefs' version has more detail about Tekanawí:ta's background, which had evolved considerably since Horatio Hale heard the story. Here is what the chiefs had to say about Tekanawí:ta, given here as *Dekanahwideh*:

The peculiar beginning of the Great Peace, or the Great League of the Five Nations at a time most ancient, is here told.

The name of the place mentioned as the birthplace of Dekanahwideh was called Kah-ha-nah-yenh, somewhere in the neighborhood of the Bay of Quinte.

According to tradition, a woman was living in that neighborhood who had one daughter of stainless character who did not travel away from home, but remained with her mother constantly, and when she had attained the age of womanhood she had held no manner of intercourse with any man. In the course of time, notwithstanding, she showed signs of conception and her mother was very much aggrieved. The mother, therefore, spoke to her daughter and said: "I am going to ask you a question and I want you to tell me the truth. What has happened to you and how is it that you are going to bear a child?" Then the daughter replied and said, "Mother I will tell you the truth, I do not know how I became with child."

Then the mother said: "The reply you give me is not sufficient to remove my grief. I am sure that you did not tell me the full truth concerning what I asked you." Then the daughter replied: "I have indeed told you the whole truth concerning what you asked me." Then the sorrowing mother said: "Of a truth, my daughter, you have no love for me."

Then she began to ill-treat her daughter, and then the daughter also began to feel aggrieved, because of this ill-treatment from her mother.

It so happened that as the time approached when the daughter would deliver the child, that the mother dreamed that she saw a man whom she did not know, and that he said that he appeared as a messenger to her on account of her troubled mind, caused by the condition of her daughter who had in so mysterious a manner conceived a child.

"I am here to deliver to you a message and now I will ask you to cease your grieving and trouble of mind, and the ill-treatment of your daughter from day to day because it is indeed a fact that your daughter does not know how she became with child. I will tell you what has happened. It is the wish of the Creator that she should bear a child, and when you will see the male child you shall call him Dekanahwideh. The reason you shall give him that name is because this child will reveal to men-beings (Ong'weonwe'), the Good Tidings of Peace and Power from Heaven, and the Great Peace shall rule and govern on earth, and I will charge you that you and your daughter should be kind to him because he has an important mission to perform in the world, and when he grows up to be a man do not prevent him from leaving home."

Then the old woman, (Iagen'tci) asked the messenger, what office the child should hold.

The messenger answered and said: "His mission is for peace and life to the people both on earth and in heaven."

When the old woman woke up the next morning she spoke to her daughter and said: "My daughter, I ask you to pardon me for all the ill-treatment I have given you because I have now been satisfied that you told me the truth when you told me that you did not know how you got the child which you are about to deliver."

Then the daughter also was made glad, and when she was delivered of the child, it was as had been predicted; the child was a male child, and the grandmother called him Dekanahwideh.[69]

The narrative of the chiefs' committee goes on to describe the remarkable signs that Tekanawí:ta employs, including the canoe that he carves from white rock:

> The child grew up rapidly, and when he had become a young man he said: "The time has come when I should begin to perform my duty in this world. I will therefore begin to build my canoe and by tomorrow I must have it completed because there is work for me to do tomorrow when I go away to the eastward."

> Then he began to build his canoe out of a white rock, and when he had completed it, Dekanahwideh said: "I am ready now to go away from home and I will tell you that there is a tree on top of the hill and you shall have that for a sign whenever you wish to find out whether I shall be living or dead. You will take an axe and chop the tree and if the tree flows blood from the cut, you will thereby know that I am beheaded and killed, but if you find no blood running from this tree after you have chopped a chip from it, then you may know that my mission was successful. The reason that this will happen is because I came to stop forever the wanton shedding of blood among human beings."

> Then Dekanahwideh also said: "Come to the shore of the lake and see me start away."

> So his mother and his grandmother went together with him and helped to pull the boat to the lake and as they stood at the lake, Dekanahwideh said: "Good bye, my mothers, for I am about to leave you for I am to go for a long time. When I return I will not come this way."

> Then the grandmother said "How are you going to travel since your canoe is made out of stone. It will not float."

Then Dekanahwideh said, "This will be the first sign of wonder that man will behold; a canoe made out of stone will float."

Then he bade them farewell, put his canoe in the lake and got in. Then he paddled away to the eastward and the grand-mother and his mother with wonder beheld him and saw that his canoe was going swiftly. In a few moments he disappeared out of their sight.

It happened at that time a party of hunters had a camp on the south side of the lake now known as Ontario and one of the party went toward the lake and stood on the bank of the lake, and beheld the object coming toward him at a distance, and the man could not understand what it was that was approaching him; shortly afterwards he understood that it was a canoe, and saw a man in it, and the moving object was coming directly toward where he stood, and when the man (it was Dekanahwideh) reached the shore he came out of his boat and climbed up the bank.

Then Dekanahwideh asked the man what had caused them to be where they were, and the man answered and said: "We are here for a double object. We are here hunting game for our living and also because there is a great strife in our settlement."

Then Dekanahwideh said, "You will now return to the place from whence you came. The reason that this occurs is because the Good Tidings of Peace and Friendship have come to the people, and you will find all strife removed from your settle-ment when you go back to your home. And I want you to tell your chief that the Ka-rih-wi-yoh (Good Tidings of Peace and Power) have come and if he asks you from whence came the Good Tidings of Peace and Power, you will say that the Messenger of the Good Tidings of Peace and Power will come in a few days.

Then the man said: "Who are you now speaking to me?" Dekanahwideh answered: "It is I who came from the west and am going eastward and am called Dekanahwideh in the world."

Then the man wondered and beheld his canoe and saw that his canoe was made out of white stone.[70]

Newhouse's version, which appears as "The Dekanawida Legend" in Parker's monograph, contains a number of significant differences from the chiefs' version.

First, it identifies Tekanawí:ta's people as Hurons, or "Crooked Tongues," who reject him because of his handsome face and good mind: "Their hearts were bitter against a man who loved not war better than all things."[71] The committee of chiefs' version makes no mention of his tribal affiliation or of any contact with anyone other than his mother and grandmother.

Second, Newhouse has Tekanawí:ta's grandmother attempt to kill him three times by pushing him into a hole in the ice. In the chief's version, a messenger comes to her in a dream before any attempt is made to harm the child. (A 1984 version has the old woman drowning him, burning him, and then planning to hack him up with a hatchet before the spirit intervenes![72])

Third, Newhouse's version has no mention of a mystical stone canoe, which figures prominently in the chief's version. How he got across Lake Ontario is left to the imagination.

Chief John Arthur Gibson, a member of the committee of chiefs, must not have been satisfied with the committee's final results, because he recorded his own version of the confederation epic. Here is how the English translation of his text begins:

This is what happened when it originated, the Great Law. This is what happened in ancient times: There was warfare, and they habitually killed each other, the Indians of the several nations. This is what was going on: They scalped one another at the various settlements, that is, the warriors were roaming about across the bush, scalping the inhabitants. Moreover, this was happening where the Mohawks resided, at the lake shore, on the northerly side of the lake, Lake Ontario, which is where a mother lived with her daughter...[73]

Thus we have Tekanawí:ta going from Mohawk to Huron and back to Mohawk again, and getting a slick new canoe in the process, not to mention an aboriginal claim to some of the best fishing in Ontario.

Now you know why we have a *living history*.

Tradition identifies Tyendinaga's Eagle Hill as the birthplace of the Peacemaker.
(Photo by Jacob Thompson)

13

WILDERNESS MESSIAH

In the introductory notes that accompanied the chiefs' version of the Peacemaker story, signed by Six Nations Council Secretary Josiah Hill and Mohawk Chief J. W. M. Elliot, we find this statement:

With reference to the origin or birth, character, and doings of Dekanahwideh as herein chronicled, it will be observed that they present an analogy or similarity to Hebrew biblical history and teachings. This is portrayed strongly in the narration of the birth of Dekanahwideh and also in certain extraordinary powers which he is attributed to have possessed.

There is little doubt that some of this influence was brought about as a result of the labors and teachings of the Jesuit fathers among them. In the early discovery of the Five Nations the Jesuit fathers made an effort to christianize them.

These precepts as taught and inculcated in the minds of the people by these missionaries have been assimilated to some extent and wrought into their own religious belief, as well perhaps into the story of the traditional nativity of this founder of the Iroquois Confederacy.[74]

The emergence of Tekanawí:ta as the central character of the confederation epic in the late 19th and early 20th centuries is hardly a case of Jesus sneaking in through the back door, as the most jaded observer might conclude.

Undoubtedly, Christian teachings may have had some influence on the evolution of the confederation epic in the literature. Seth Newhouse didn't learn to read and write from looking at cereal boxes; Christian missionaries probably had a hand in his education. The same holds true for the committee of chiefs, who acknowledged the possibility of influence in their introduction. They also state that their document was to be presented to the Canadian government to prevent the arrival of officials to conduct elections. Perhaps giving Tekanawí:ta Christ-like attributes may have been a subtle way of saying, "Keep your missionaries away, too! We've already got a Jesus."

We must not forget that the virgin birth of Tekanawí:ta has precedents not only in Christianity, but also in our creation story. Just as an earlier Onondaga version linked Aionwà:tha to Teharonhiawá:kon, the later confederation accounts make the same connection to Tekanawí:ta by recasting Sky Woman and her virgin daughter as Tekanawí:ta's grandmother and mother. Like the twins of creation, he is the product of both flesh and spirit. Therein lies the beauty of a matrilineal society: you always know who your mother is, but your father can be anybody— including the supernatural.

Dutch colonist Johannes Megapolensis heard the story of Sapling and Flint in the 1640's and assumed we were only regurgitating Cain and Abel. We would be wise not to assume that when we hear the story of Tekanawí:ta, we are simply hearing an Iroquois version of the New Testament. Instead, we are witnessing a people paying homage to their most ancient beliefs by giving them new life, new meaning. We are witnessing the workings of a living culture and a living history.

That being said, Christian teachings *did* have an influence on the development of the league tradition, as noted by the words of the late Cayuga chief, Jake Thomas, one of the confederacy's most respected keepers of traditional lore:

...the elders feel that the Peacemaker made the Laws and united the nations before he went across the great salt water to the land of the white race. We feel that it was the same prophet that the white race call Jesus as he was reborn again from a virgin mother and gave the white race the good tidings of peace on earth. So this is according to the elders and what they talked about the founding of the League more than three thousand years ago.[75]

It is not surprising that a similar "intrusion" occurred among the communities that were traditionally Catholic. *Kanehsatà:ke*, the Mohawk community at the Lake of Two Mountains west of Montreal, would have been somewhat peripheral to events taking place at the Grand River, but they too incorporated a Jesus figure into their folklore. An example of this is found in *At The Woods' Edge: An Anthology of the History of the People of Kanehsatake* (1995):

Here is a very old legend from the elders of Kanehsata:ke. At that time there was a clan of Onkwehon:we, they were hunters, settled at some place. At this time, different nations of Indians were having battles among different nations. This happened about 1,900 years ago.

These Onkwehon:we were nomadic, they would travel all over the place hunting and living off the land. All of a sudden this man appeared to them. He was dressed in a white robe. He told them that it was not right the Indians were battling against Indians, that it was not right that brothers should fight. These Indians were very angry and they all had their spears and arrows pointed at this man who appeared to them and they were ready to kill him. But they did not do this to him.

He said to them, "You did not kill me, this clan of Indians who are living here. This place that I went to over the Great Waters, they killed me." The Indians were very afraid. He showed them where they had wounded him. His right hand and his left hand were pierced, he also had a wound on his chest. The Indians were truly amazed that a man could be this wounded and he wasn't dead.

The Onkwehon:we believed it was not right that they should battle and fight among themselves. He said to them that he did not like for them to put on their war paint and kill each other because they were brothers. He then made a sweeping motion with his right hand and there appeared in front of the Indians a clear creek. He told them to wash the war paint from their faces. They listened and every man cleansed himself. When they finished washing themselves they were amazed to find that the creek, which had been crystal clear water, had turned the colour of blood.

This man said to the Indians that he was leaving now and that he was going to visit the other tribes. This was what happened. He was there and then he disappeared just the way he had appeared to them in the first place.[76]

Tales of Jesus-like prophets appear to be common among tribes of the entire western hemisphere. In 1963, L. Tayler Hansen published a survey of these "pale god" myths, *He Walked the Americas*. This is where we find the following tradition by "Chief Big Tree" of the Senecas, who shared this "apocryphal" story in the 1920's:

Once while in the Capitol City, the Prophet heard tales of the Sunrise Ocean and the Five Tribes of Warring Nations. At once He expressed a desire to see them, for much opposed to war was the Healer, so He went forth with the merchants. Across the mighty Alleghenies the Pale God came to the Seneca Nation. There He called the Chieftains into Council.

Long He spoke to them on the ways of His Father, as He had throughout the Broad Land, handling the language with great ease. He explained His Peace Religion, then He asked of them quite simply: what was the reason for their warfare? The Fire Chieftains were embarrassed, for they had long forgotten the reason, if indeed they ever had a reason. Each warrior looked upon the other and none could think of a valid answer.

Therefore He bound them ceremonially into a never-ending alliance. To each He gave a sacred duty to perform for the alliance, and then He asked them to smoke the Peace Pipe, filled with tobacco and cedar shavings, and to blow the smoke to the four directions making the sign of the Great Cross, which is a holy symbol.

Never from that time onward have the Five Nations fought each other, nor has the trust He gave them been cracked or broken.

At this Council was a Seneca Chieftain who was tall, for we are a tall nation. Like many of our people he had a lofty stature, and could easily look down on the heads of the others. Indeed the Prophet was not a short man, but neither was He as tall as the Chieftain. The Seneca, seeing that he was the tallest, and could look over the light hair of the Pale God, rose and waited to speak.

There was a shocked silence. Would he presume to question the Prophet?

The Chieftain looked upon the Healer.

'I have been watching you while you were speaking, oh One whom the people call the Dawn God. It is true that you hold a most strange fascination over the minds of men. I know that the people call you the Dawn God. If it is true, then you can prove it. Meet me here in four days in the early morning before the sun has shot his first long red arrow, and we shall stand before this door together. If the first red arrow of the dawn light, touches your hair before it paints my feather, then indeed you are the Dawn God. This I give to you as a challenge. Now, for this day, I have spoken.'

Everyone turned to look at the prophet. He sat quite still as if in deep thought. At last He arose.

'Your stand is well taken. I will meet you here before the dawning. When the Sunrise Ocean arises the golden light of the Dawn Star, I will be standing here before the Great Lodge. I will use up the moments of waiting to talk once more with the People — all who would care to hear me. For now, I too have spoken.'

During the four days the Healer went among the tribes, and though He did not speak of His appointment, everyone knew that He would keep it, for the Great One never broke a promise.

Accordingly, at the time appointed, great crowds swarmed about the small mound where the Great Lodge stood open to the eastward. First to climb the mound was the Prophet. As over the horizon arose the first golden shafts of the Dawn Star, the Pale God spoke to the assembled nations. It is said that He always charmed His listeners, but now there was almost a breathless silence. Indeed it seemed the very trees were listening and also the assembled animals of the forest, so softly He spoke and so well did they hear Him, because of the silence that had settled.

Now the tall chieftain left the others and slowly climbed the small mound, taking his place beside the Prophet. The two eagle feathers in the hair of the chieftain projected well above the head of the Healer, but no sign except a friendly greeting was given by the Pale Hea-wah-sah, who turned and began the Chant of the Dawning. This was a Prayer Chant He had taught the people, which has long since been forgotten. Everyone started to join in and then, suddenly, a miracle happened.

Before anyone else saw the sunlight, a golden shaft of radiant beauty came down from some clouds banked high with fire-light, and touched the curling hair of the Prophet, diffusing itself like a halo until He stood, a luminous creature, painting all the ground around Him with gold.

The people then fell down saying: 'Behold He is indeed the Dawn God who has come to walk among us!' and 'He draws his power from the Star of the Dawning.'

The tall chieftain, seeing the Great One clothed in gold light, knelt in the dust beside Him and taking the hem of the Prophet's mantle, laid his cheek on the line of creases.

I know that you think this sounds something like the Legend of Hiawatha written down by Longfellow, the poet. You are right; there is a resemblance. Once he was our guest and heard us chanting. He liked our stories so well that he kept urging us onward through his interpreter of the language. We told him many stories. When he returned and began to write them, he mixed them all together; but he was not trying to make fun of our legends — he was confused. We still honor him for enjoying the chants, and even trying to get the rhythm of their language. We honor him although Hea-wah-sah never sought a Dacotah maiden. That was a much later hero, who married with a distant nation.

The meaning of Hea-wah-sah? It is He From Afar Off. It is our name for the Prophet, who drew His great strength from the Dawn Star. All nations know He was of the Dawn Star, and that is why, even now, no nation of the ancient people known as 'red-skins' will ever make war or fight a battle while the Sacred Star of Peace is still shining in the great heavens. They dare not, for it is the Star of the Prophet.[77]

Chief Big Tree places a "pale god" at the heart of confederation, but it should be kept in mind that this was not the only version the Seneca had. They also told the story in a way that was quite faithful to the old way of telling it, with Tekanawí:ta as a normal but weary Mohawk chief. This was consistent with a version told by the Onondagas who also remained in the United States. At the Six Nations Reserve, however, the story seemed to suddenly flourish…as if its roots had found fertile soil on the banks of the Grand River.

It seems obvious that the creation story was an influence on the way the story evolved, but the Christian influence will probably be debated forever. What other influences may have played a part in the regeneration of this story?

14

A MISCHIEF MAKER AMONG THE WYANDOTS

The transformation of a Mohawk chief into the virgin-born Huron Peacemaker wasn't influenced by Christian teachings alone. There was another influence that had nothing at all to do with the colonists and their missionaries, but was indigenous in origin.

As we saw in a previous chapter, a 19th century version of the confederation epic mentions a northern threat that motivated the Five Nations to unite.

> Suddenly there arose a great alarm at the invasion of a ferocious band of warriors from the north of the Great Lakes.[78]

Who were these people? Looking northward, there are many Iroquoian and Algonquian peoples in the running, but the likely suspects are the mighty Hurons. As Fenton says:

> …the Iroquois tradition in Ontario is much earlier than previously thought. This all gives credence to the Huron tradition that their confederacy was formed starting at the mid-fifteenth century, and the Iroquois confederacy could not have been far behind.[79]

In the 17th century, the Huron Confederacy lived in the area between Georgian Bay and Lake Simcoe, just east of Lake Huron. There were five nations in their alliance: *Attignawantan*, *Attigneenongnahac*, *Arendaronon*, *Tahontaenrat*, and *Ataronchronon*. They knew themselves collectively as *Ouendat*, or *Wendat*,[80] sometimes rendered as *Wyandot*.

You will recall that in the late 19th century, Seth Newhouse identified the Peacemaker's people as Hurons living on the Bay of Quinte, on the north shore of Lake Ontario. Tuscarora scholar J. N. B. Hewitt took credit for supplying this information to Newhouse. Newhouse then incorporated it into his written account of the Tekanawí:ta legend. According to Hewitt:

> The source of the utter confusion of names and places probably arose from misunderstanding certain information which the present writer many years ago gave to Mr. Newhouse concerning the early inhabitants of what is now Ontario, Canada. This information contained the suggestion that Dekanawida was very probably a naturalized Huron captive among the Iroquois.[81]

Today, it is almost universally accepted among Iroquois traditionalists that the Peacemaker was a Huron, owing perhaps to the prominence of the Newhouse version in the literature. (Although they deny it, they all have a dog-eared copy of *Parker on the Iroquois* somewhere in their house!)

Joseph Brant believed that Hurons did at one time live at the Bay of Quinte, according to family traditions he shared with Teyoninhogarawen. These stories suggests that there may be more to Newhouse's "Huron" Peacemaker story than Hewitt realized.

> The late Colonel Brant, Thayendanegea, (who is descended from Wyandot prisoners adopted by the Mohawks both on the father and mother's side,) told me, that his Grandmother was taken prisoner, when the Wyandots inhabited the country about the Bay of Quinty, on the northern shore of Lake Ontario; and gave the following account of the preceeding tokens and causes of the War between that Nation and the Mohawk Confederates.

Brant's first story takes place "while the Sun shone in peace on their respective Villages; fore the gloom of war had clouded the horizon." A Wyandot man and his son camp out near the grave of a dead warrior, whose ghost awakens them with the singing of his war song. The man sends his son away while he faces the ghost in battle. The ghost kills him and chases the boy, who manages to escape by hiding in a hollowed log. The ghost breaks his ax trying to get at the boy. The next morning the villagers dig up the grave of the warrior and find the broken ax lying there with his bones.

Norton recorded another of Brant's "ominous" tales:

A young man of the Wyandots, in the evening, after he had retired to his birth, was roused by a rap given on the outside of the house, opposite to where he lay, which, as it was of bark, revibrated through. The rap was followed by the voice of a Man, which said, 'Are you not invited to the feast given by your father's relation?' The young man answered, 'No, I did not hear of any feast that they had made.' 'Yes, (continued the stranger,) and if you get up in the morning and go to the other end of the village you will see the place.' In the morning, as soon as the young man arose, curiosity urged him to go and examine the place mentioned by the voice, and there he found appearances corroborate the truth of what had been told to him: he saw where they had danced, and the half burnt logs where they had had the fire. He felt, seriously, the affront of having been neglected by his paternal kindred. (For it is a universal custom with the Nottowegui race, that the paternal relations shew every mark of respect and tenderness to the children of their male kindred, although they do not consider them so near of kin as those of the female line), however he shewed no resentment, nor even took notice of it. The next night, he heard a rap again, opposite to where he lay, and a voice, saying 'Are you not now invited?' He answered, 'No, who is it that gives a feast now?' 'It is your paternal relations,' replied the stranger. He then delineated the spot, telling him to go there in the morning, and that he would see the remaining appearances of where they had danced, and where they had feasted. He went there accordingly, and found the tokens, in every respect, confirming what the stranger had told him.

He now became displeased, because he could not account for this second omission in any other manner than as proceeding from wilful neglect. His accustomed cheerfulness and gaiety forsook him; he was silent and melancholy with his companions; a sullen gloom overspread his countenance. At last, one of his comrades perceiving this change in his friend, insisted on knowing the cause of his appearing so unhappy. After repeated entreaties, he informed him: the other immediately contradicted the report, assuring him that there had been no such feast. He then led him to the place where he had found the appearances of recent festivity, corroborating the information; his friend saw these striking emblems, and made the affair known to the paternal relations, who protested that they had made no such feast, while many others were also ready to testify. They were alarmed at this attempt to make mischief between relations, and at night placed sentinels all around the Village to seize upon any stranger, that should approach it, at the time when he who made the false report was wont to come.

The people of the Village all assembled in Council, to see who this stranger might be, who had so artfully laboured to foment ill will between kindred. The warriors who had been placed on the watch, at last brought him into the Council House. The majestic stature and dignified appearance of the stranger attracted general attention; he was seated near the venerable Chiefs, who were about to interrogate him, as to the cause of his nocturnal visits, and of the method he had taken to render the young man displeased with his paternal relations, when some hasty, stupid fellow, placed among the warriors, arose, saying, 'Are you the mischief maker?' 'Take that,' giving him a blow on the nostrils; a few drops of blood fell to the ground. The stranger then said, 'I intended to have made choice of you; but you have insulted me. I shall go to another,' and instantaneously disappeared: leaving the whole assembly in surprise and dread. This, they say was Teharonghyawago, who had intended to have rendered the Wyandots, his most favored Nation in war, but who from this blow was induced to go to the side of the Five Nations, Rodinoncione.[82]

Here we have Brant's contribution to the evolving Peacemaker mythology with the story of a "mischief maker" among the Wyandots of the Bay of Quinte, identified as *Teharonghyawago*, the "good twin" of the creation story. It is implied that after this harsh treatment by the Wyandots, he went to the Iroquois…to unify them, perhaps?

It's not as crazy as it sounds. In fact, there is evidence to suggest that nothing less than an Iroquoian *trixter* has been at work in the evolving story of the Peacemaker. A Seneca legend of the "The Mischief Maker" appeared in—of all places—a book of Algonquian legends published in 1883.[83] It is given here as found in William Beauchamp's *Iroquois Folk Lore* under the title, "The Peacemaker." I will leave it up to you to decide if this is our suspect.

The Mischief Maker was pursued by some on whom he had played his pranks and took refuge in a tall and thick tree. They could not find him but built a fire and camped under this tree. The smoke crept through the branches and went straight to the sky. "The fugitive sailed away on the smoke, going up and up—past beautiful lakes and hunting grounds stocked with deer, large fields of corn and beans, tobacco and squashes; past great companies of handsome Indians, whose wigwams were hung full of dried venison and bear's meat. And so he went on and up to the wigwam of the Great Chief."

For a hundred moons he stayed there, learning a new language and habits of life. So well did he like these that he had no wish to go back when told he must do so. The Great Chief told him that he had been allowed to come that he might return and tell what he had seen. Then, if he lived aright, he might return and hunt and fish there forever.

"A cloud of smoke, in the form of a great eagle, came to him, and, seated on its back, he was borne down to the top of the tree from which he had risen. He opened his eyes. The sun was shining. His pursuers had gone away. He descended and traveled on. His mind was filled with what he had seen. He said, 'I will no longer play tricks, but tell people what I learned in the happy hunting grounds.' After a long time he drew near to a village. He gave the common signal. Runners came to meet him. The head chief and all the people came to hear. He was asked, 'What news do you bring us?' He said, 'I, that was the Mischief Maker, am the Peace Maker now,' and he told his errand.

There was great rejoicing, as he told of Ha-wen-ne-yu and his assistants. All the people might live and be happy if they would. Their Great Ruler would care for them, but they were to avoid his wicked brother, the Evil Mind. He-no was sent to do them good and had a pouch full of thunderbolts for the wicked. The Indians were to pray to him at seed time and thank him in the harvest. He was to be called Grandfather. Ga-oh was the Wind Spirit. He moved the winds, though he was chained to a rock. When he struggles the winds are forced away from him. When he is quiet they also rest. Beans, corn and squashes have each loving spirits. In fact all things have these assistant spirits, and they were to be thankful for the good work of all.

"So the Peace Maker taught the people. They threw tobacco on the fire, according to his instructions, and on the column of its smoke he was borne away to the happy hunting grounds. And the people danced and sang around the dying embers of the council fire."[84]

15

TRANSPLANTING THE ROOTS

The transformation of Tekanawí:ta from Mohawk chief to Huron mystic born of a virgin appears to have been a "Grand River" phenomenon, because the Iroquois who stayed behind in the United States retained a league tradition consistent with earlier versions. We find one example in *Seneca Myths and Folk Tales* (1923). Arthur C. Parker presents "The Origin of the Long House" as related by Delos B. Kittle, or "Chief Big Kittle," at the Cattaraugus reservation in January of 1905:

Where the Mohawk river empties into the Hudson in ancient times there was a Mohawk village. The people there were fierce and warlike and were continually sending out war parties against other settlements and returning would bring back long strings of scalps to number the lives they had destroyed. But sometimes they left their own scalps behind and never returned. They loved warfare better than all other things and were happy when their hands were slimy with blood. They boasted that they would eat up all other nations and so they continued to go against other tribes and fight with them.

Now among the Mohawks was a chief named Dekanawi'da, a very wise man, and he was very sad of heart because his people loved war too well. So he spoke in council and implored them to desist lest they perish altogether but the young warriors would not hear him and laughed at his words but he did not cease to warn them until at last dispairing of moving them by ordinary means he turned his face to the west and wept as he journeyed onward and away from his people. At length he reached a lake whose shores were fringed with bushes, and being tired he lay down to rest. Presently, as he lay meditating, he heard the soft spattering of water sliding from a skillful paddle and peering out from his hiding place he saw in the red light of sunset a man leaning over his canoe and dipping into the shallow water with a basket. When he raised it up it was full of shells, the shells of the periwinkles that live in shallow pools. The man pushed his canoe toward the shore and sat down on the beach where he kindled a fire. Then he began to string his shells and finishing a string would touch the shells and talk. Then, as if satisfied, he would lay it down and make another until he had a large number. Dekanawida watched the strange proceeding with wonder. The sun had long since set but Dekanawida still watched the man with the shell strings sitting in the flickering light of the fire that shadowed the bushes and shimmered over the lake.

After some deliberation he called out, "Kwe, I am a friend!" and stepping out upon the sand stood before the man with the shells. "I am Dekanawida," he said, "and come from the Mohawk."

"I am Haio'went'ha of the Onondaga," came the reply.

The Dekanawida inquired about the shell strings for he was very curious to know their import and Haio'went'ha answered, "They are the rules of life and laws of good government. This all white string is a sign of truth, peace and good will, this black string is a sign of hatred, of war and of a bad heart, the string with the alternate beads, black and white, is a sign that peace should exist between the nations. This string with white on either end and black in the middle is a sign that wars must end and peace declared." And so Haiowentha lifted his strings and read the laws.

Then said Dekanawida, "You are my friend indeed, and the friend of all nations.Our people are weak from warring and weak from being warred upon. We who speak one tongue should combine against the Hadindas instead of helping them by killing one another but my people are weary of my advising and would not hear me."

"I, too, am of the same mind," said Haiowentha, "but Tatodaho slew all my brothers and drove me away. So I came to the lakes and have made the laws that should govern men and nations. I believe that we should be as brothers in a family instead of enemies."

"Then come with me," said Dekanawida, "and together let us go back to my people and explain the rules and laws."

So when they had returned Dekanawida called a council of all the chiefs and warriors and the women and Haiowentha set forth the plan he had devised. The words had a marvelous effect. The people were astonished at the wisdom of the strange chief from the Onondaga and when he had finished his exposition the chiefs promised obedience to his laws. They delegated Dekanawida to go with him to the Oneida and council with them, then to go onward to Onondaga and win over the arrogant erratic Tatodaho, the tyrannical chief of the Onondaga. Thus it was that together they went to the Oneida country and won over their great chief and made the people promise to support the proposed league. Then the Oneida went with Haiowentha to the Cayugas and told them how by supporting the league they might preserve themselves against the fury of Tatodaho. So when the Cayuga had promised allegiance Dekanawida turned his face toward Onondaga and with his comrades went before Tatodaho. Now when Tatodaho learned how three nations had combined against him he became very angry and ran into the forest where he gnawed at his fingers and ate grass and leaves. His evil thoughts became serpents and sprouted from his skull and waving in a tangled mass hissed out venom. But Dekanawida did not fear him and once more asked him to give his consent to a league of peace and friendship but he was still wild until Haiowentha combed the snakes from his head and told him that he should be the head chief of the confederacy and govern it according to the laws that Haiowentha had made. Then he recovered from his madness and asked why the Seneca had not been visited for the Seneca outnumbered all the other nations and were fearless warriors. "If their jealousy is aroused," he said, "they will eat us."

Then the delegation visited the Seneca and the other nations to the west but only the Seneca would consider the proposal. The other nations were exceedingly jealous.

Thus a peace pact was made and the Long House built and Dekanawida was the builder but Haiowentha was its designer.[85]

Chief Big Kittle was a contemporary of Seth Newhouse and John Arthur Gibson, but his version of the story is consistent with what was captured by Joseph Brant and John Norton about a century before. The only supernatural element is the snakes growing out of the skull of the evil Onondaga chief, Atotárho. Tekanawí:ta is still a Mohawk chief. Aionwà:tha has a canoe, but no mention is made of it being carved out of stone or anything out of the ordinary.

So what was it about life at the Six Nations reserve in the 19th century that inspired such a profound regeneration of the legend? Was it the few extra days of winter? When storytellers had extra time to kill, did they feel free to stretch their creative muscles?

A more likely story is that the descendents of the Iroquois who moved to Canada after the American Revolution needed to culturally connect themselves to their new location, so they unconsciously searched the storyteller's pouch for something to link them to the Bay of Quinte— and remembered the stories Joseph Brant had told them about a "mischief maker" among the Wyandots who once lived there.

By transplanting Tekanawí:ta's roots in the heart of a new "Mohawk country," and by reaffirming his connection to the Teharonhiawá:kon from the creation story, they were telling their new neighbors that not only were they *not* immigrants to these lands, but that they were restoring to themselves the "holiest of holies," the most sacred place in all of Iroquoia—the birthplace of their god!

If you visit Tyendinaga, you may be taken to a hill overlooking a marsh where it is believed the Peacemaker's birth narrative took place. When I first visited Tyendinaga many years before I began this research, I could not help but sense the sacredness of the place. I have recently returned there to find that this feeling hasn't been diminished by the things I've learned in my research. If anything, it has grown stronger with time.

16

THE GLOOSKAP LEGENDS

As we consider the possibility that the legend of the Peacemaker evolved over time to include his virgin birth and his carving of a canoe out of stone, we must also concede the possibility that there was no such evolution, and that we're really only talking about alternate versions of the story that simply hadn't been captured at an earlier time, but may be just as old.

Were he still alive today, we would have a hard time convincing J. N. B. Hewitt of that. He was very familiar with the late 19th century versions of the story that emphasize those concepts. In his review of Arthur C. Parker's publication of those versions, he expressed his doubts about the "truth" of the stone canoe:

> It is noteworthy that the Secretaries of the Committee of Chiefs of the Six Nations Council admit that the traditions which they recorded have been "much modified" by several causes. But these annalists failed to detect in some notable instances the elements which have been assimilated by the League traditions from their mythic and other tales. Such, for example, are the following: the notion of "the white stone canoe" or the "marble canoe," and the "Ohsinoh" incidents. Now, the "stone" or "flint" canoe belongs to the cycle of stories which relate to the Winter God whose means of travel on water is a block of ice, which is poetically transformed into a "canoe." So this episode does not belong to the Dekanawida legend. Mr. J.V.H. Clarke (Onondaga, 1, 1849) records the Dekanawida story, but he writes "white canoe" only; the original Dekanawida canoe was probably a birchbark canoe. But tradition has expanded "white" into "white stone" as suggested above.[86]

Neither Hewitt nor Parker mention that the stone canoe was prominent in the legends of other tribes, particularly the Mi'kmaq and others of the Algonquian language group. As anthropologists, they certainly should have been aware of Charles G. Leland's *Algonquin Legends of New England, or, Myths and Folk Lore of the Micmac, Passamaquoddy, and Penobscot Tribes*, published in 1884—more than 30 years before Parker's monograph.

Many of the legends Leland recounts are about *Glooskap*, an archetypical hero reminiscent of Teharonhiawá:kon of the Iroquois creation story. The first of these is titled, "Of Glooskap's Birth, and of his Brother Malsum the Wolf."

Now the great lord Glooskap, who was worshiped in after-days by all the Wabanaki, or children of light, was a twin with a brother. As he was good, this brother, whose name was Malsumsis, or Wolf the younger, was bad. Before they were born, the babes consulted to consider how they had best enter the world. And Glooskap said, "I will be born as others are." But the evil Malsumsis thought himself too great to be brought forth in such a manner, and declared that he would burst through his mother's side. And as they planned it so it came to pass. Glooskap as first came quietly to light, while Malsumsis kept his word, killing his mother.

The two grew up together, and one day the younger, who knew that both had charmed lives, asked the elder what would kill him, Glooskap. Now each had his own secret as to this, and Glooskap, remembering how wantonly Malsumsis had slain their mother, thought it would be misplaced confidence to trust his life to one so fond of death, while it might prove to be well to know the bane of the other. So they agreed to exchange secrets, and Glooskap, to test his brother, told him that the only way in which he himself could be slain was by the stroke of an owl's feather, though this was not true. And Malsumsis said, "I can only die by a blow from a fern-root."

It came to pass in after-days that Kwah-beet-a-sis, the son of the Great Beaver, or, as others say, Miko the Squirrel, or else the evil which was in himself, tempted Malsumsis to kill Glooskap; for in those days all men were wicked. So taking his bow he shot Ko-ko-khas the Owl, and with one of his feathers he struck Glooskap while sleeping. Then he awoke in anger, yet craftily said that it was not by an owl's feather, but by a blow from a pine-root, that his life would end.

Then the false man led his brother another day far into the forest to hunt, and, while he again slept, smote him on the head with a pine-root. But Glooskap arose unharmed, drove Malsumsis away into the woods, sat down by the brook-side, and thinking aver all that had happened, said, "Nothing but a flowering rush can kill me." But the Beaver, who was hidden among the reeds, heard this, and hastening to Malsumsis told him the secret of his brother's life. For this Malsumsis promised to bestow on Beaver whatever he should ask; but when the latter wished for wings like a pigeon, the warrior laughed, and scornfully said, "Get thee hence; thou with a tail like a file, what need hast thou of wings?"

Then the Beaver was angry, and went forth to the camp of Glooskap, to whom he told what he had done. Therefore Glooskap arose in sorrow and in anger, took a fern-root, sought Malsumsis in the deep, dark forest, and smote him so that he fell down dead. And Glooskap sang a song over him and lamented.

The Beaver and the Owl and the Squirrel, for what they did and as they did it, all come again into these stories; but Malsumsis, being dead, was turned into the Shick-shoe mountains in the Gaspe peninsula.

For this chapter and parts of others I am indebted to the narrative of a Micmac Indian, taken down by Mr. Edward Jock; also to another version in the Rand MS. The story is, in the main-points, similar to that given by David Cusick in his

History of the Six Nations, of Enigorio the Good Mind, and Enigonhahetgea, Bad Mind, to which I shall refer anon.

It is very evident that in this tradition Glooskap represents the Good principle, and Malsumsis, the little wolf,—that is the Wolf who is the Younger, rather than little or small,—the Evil one. Malsum typifies destruction and sin in several of these tales. He will arise at the last day, when Glooskap is to do battle with all the giants and evil beasts of olden time, and will be the great destroyer.[87]

In other stories recounted by Leland, Glooskap bears a striking resemblance to Tekanawí:ta, the Peacemaker of the Iroquois. Like Tekanawí:ta, Glooskap travels about in a stone canoe. He even takes a voyage to the "old world." We find this in the Passamaquoddy legend, "How Glooskap went to England and France, and was the first to make America known to the Europeans."[88]

The Mi'kmaq have a story in which an evil wizard goads Glooskap into battle by capturing two girls at spear point and forcing them into Glooskap's stone canoe. After rescuing the girls, Glooskap overturns the canoe with the wizard in it. The broken canoe becomes the Bird Islands in St. Ann's Bay at Cape Breton, Nova Scotia.[89]

The Abenaki call this culture hero *Gluskab* or *Gluskabe*. Their stories mention his stone canoe as well.[90] There is also a stone canoe associated with another tribe in the Algonquian family, but it has nothing to do with Glooskap.

We find it in an "old Ojibwa story" attributed to a woman named Fritz Bizhoo. "The White Canoe Made from Stone" is the story of a man who is grief-stricken when his wife dies on their wedding day. An old man tells him to follow a path to a lakeshore and take the canoe that he finds there out to an island where he will meet his wife. He goes to the lake and finds that the canoe is made of white stone, but it floats and is able to carry him to the island. He spends a week there with his wife in perfect happiness before returning to live out the rest of his days as a great leader among his people. When he dies, he has a smile on his face, knowing that he will return to his wife.[91]

So what are we to make of all this? Was the stone canoe of Algonquian folklore the inspiration for the stone canoe of the Peacemaker? Or was it the other way around? Does one legend negate the next, or do they actually confirm one another? Are they really just the common myth of neighboring tribes, or are they evidence that *somebody* paddled about in a stone canoe?

If you prefer a more academic mystery, why have the striking similarities in these Iroquoian and Algonquian cultural myths been ignored by anthropologists like Hewitt, Parker, and those who came after them? Why were these mythologies dealt with in such isolation? As next-door neighbors, these two cultural groups had thousands of years of interaction, yet scholars have treated them as if they developed on separate planets.

It has often been said that the Peacemaker's vision was that the White Roots of Peace would spread to the four corners of the world, and that all nations were welcome to follow those roots to their source and take shelter beneath the Tree of Peace. He never said that they would have to forsake their cultural identities to do so. The Great Law did not require them to take on our legends and songs as their own, and to look, speak, and act exactly like us. Perhaps this is the key to the regeneration of the Peacemaker's story that took place at the Grand River in the late 19th century: those who took shelter with us were free to share their stories, just as we were free to share ours with them. This would explain not only the influence of the Algonquian stone canoe, but the Huron identity given to the Mohawk Tekanawí:ta. Since the Iroquois were establishing a presence in what was at various times considered Huron and Algonquian territory, it made sense to include certain cultural aspects of these people in our evolving belief system, to make them feel as though they have always been a part of it. In that sense, the spreading of the White Roots of Peace would have happened in a much more subtle and peaceful manner than advocates of the "Imperial Iroquois" school of thought would have us believe.

III

THE WAMPUM CHRONICLES

17

THE GREAT BELTS OF THE LEAGUE

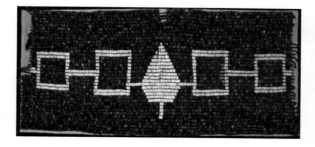

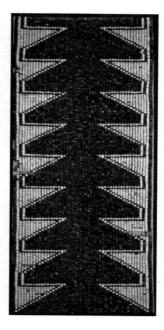

The reader by now has noticed that wampum is only briefly mentioned in the literature concerning the establishment of the Iroquois league, occurring as it did long before the advent of tubular clamshell beads of the colonial era. As many traditional people will tell you, Aionwà:tha probably used something other than cylindrical beads made from quahog and whelk shells—such as freshwater spiral shells, porcupine quills, eagle feather quills, or elderberry twigs—when he created the first condolence strings. Therefore it stands to reason that the massive wampum belts associated with confederation—namely, the Aionwà:tha, Atotárho, and Ever-growing Tree—were created as memorials long after the event, perhaps in the 17th or 18th centuries. This would also apply to the "circle wampum" which depicts the 50 chiefs of the league, and with other emblematic wampum belts and strings that are the hallmark of Iroquois diplomacy and ritual. These came after the league was founded, but long before the league tradition was shared with Europeans or written by down by our own people. They may have formed a visual "infrastructure" around which the various supernatural elements coalesced in the 19th century. It leads us to wonder if the belts are truly memorials of an ancient story—or is it the story that is a memorial to the belts?

The literature concerning the three "Great Belts of the League" is worth reviewing, as it not only parallels the collection of the various confederation epics, but reaffirms the prominence of Aionwà:tha in the league tradition. We will deal with each belt individually.

18

THE AIONWÀ:THA BELT:
THE WAMPUM THAT INSPIRED THE FLAG

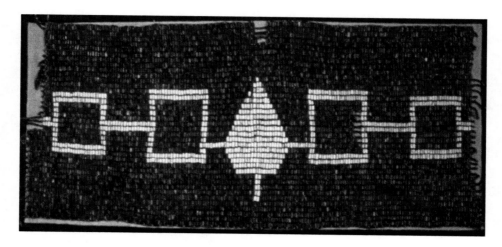

As I stated in the introduction of this book, the wampum belt named after Aionwà:tha is the universal icon of the Rotinonhsón:ni Confederacy. It's imagery was the inspiration for our modern flag.

The Aionwà:tha belt was among the collection of belts and strings shown to scholar J. V. H. Clark in 1849. He describes the Aionwà:tha belt as

> ...representing the first union of and league of the Five Nations, and is called the *carpet*, or foundation or platform, or as we may better understand it, the constitution; literally something to stand upon. The several nations are distinguished by particular squares, and these are joined together by a line of white wampum and united to a heart in the center, implying the union of heart and hand as one.[92]

E. W. Paige travelled to Onondaga in 1898 to consult with Daniel and Thomas La Fort. They told him that the

Aionwà:tha Belt represented One heart of the Five Nations—
that if any hurt of any animal would pierce that heart, then
they would all feel it—all the Five Nations. This was in *Hi-a-
wat-ha's* belt. That they are a united people. This is the
original *Hi-a-wat-ha* belt—a record of the first agreement to
make the league.[93]

William Beauchamp went into much more detail about the
Aionwà:tha belt in his study, "Wampum and Shell Articles Used by the
New York Indians," published in *The Bulletin of the New York State
Museum* in 1901:

During his knowledge of them various and conflicting interpretations of these belts have come before the writer. Some
will be given to show how little is certainly known. Fig. 252 is
the reputed original record of the formation of the league, and
the tradition is constant. Clark had this interpretation, but
exaggerated the belt's dimensions. Instead of being 4 feet long
by 16 inches broad, it was 10.5 inches wide by 23 long in 1878,
showing a great loss at each end. The width of course had not
suffered. When exhibited in Syracuse in 1886 it was said:
"This belt was used at the great council which met to ratify the
union of the Five Nations. The age is unknown; nothing
but the tradition of the council remains." Gen. Carrington,
who obtained this from the Onondagas, calls it "the official
memorial of the organization of the Iroquois confederacy,
relating back to the middle of the 16th century." It is sometimes called the Hi-a-wat-ha belt, and has been in controversy
in our courts over a question of ownership. It is a fine modern
belt of 38 rows, made on buckskin thongs, the outer ones
braided, and is strung with flax or hemp thread. The beads
were made with modern tools and are mostly purple. There is
a conventional heart in the center, and four open castles
remain in white beads. As the pattern shows that there
were others beyond these on either hand, this plainly proves
that it had no reference to the original league. It is probably

not 150 years old. There are good pictures of all in the census of 1900. Gen. Carrington was special agent for the census of 1890, and his farther notes will be credited to Thomas Donaldson, the compiler of the report on the Six Nations of New York.[94]

Like Beauchamp before him, anthropologist William Fenton wondered if the Aionwà:tha belt offered any clues to the age of the confederacy itself. But unlike Beauchamp, he had modern science to assist him in his own analysis. As he recorded in 1971:

The Hiawatha belt is most interesting on two counts: the Iroquois date it from the formation of the League, and yet it cannot be that old. This relic, which measures 21 ½ by 10 ½ inches today, is thirty-eight rows deep, and is composed of 6,916 beads, mostly purple with white figures. Its form is a mat, the warps of which are buckskin thongs, the outer ones braided, and the beads are strung as wefts on hemp thread. In the solid purple field is worked a design of white shell beads, illustrating a tree or heart, flanked by two sets of hollow squares which are connected to each other by a double row of white beads which extends to the extremities, and by a single row to the central figure. The design is self-contained, and although it is raveled and frayed at both ends, and Beauchamp states that it measured 23 inches in 1878, I do not think that it has lost many courses of beads at the ends because the fringe shows but few additional courses of wefts which end well within the fringe itself. When the mat is oriented east and west like the Longhouse of the League, with the Tree of Peace pointing north, the first two squares represent the Mohawk and Oneida nations, the Evergrowing Tree stands at Onondaga, and the third and fourth squares contain the Cayuga and Seneca nations. The path runs from the eastern door on the Schoharie to the western door of the Longhouse on the Genesee river.

The belt contains beads of several sorts, irregular in size, varying in diameter and length. The drilling, which is plain in x-ray photographs, show's two extremes of technical skill, some having been drilled from opposite ends and not meeting, while others, which are closer to the margins of the belt are drilled all the way through, presumably in one direction. Since we know that the latter technique represents an improvement on the former, it would appear that this belt must have been done over at some time, using beads from two different sources, possibly taken from two belts of differing age that were discarded by the council, as was the practice when belts were no longer needed, they were deemed unimportant to preserve, and were therefore unstrung to make new ones. If beads taken from two belts of differing age were lumped before weaving, we would expect to find them distributed at random in the tapestry. The fact that newer beads occur near the margins suggests some kind of selection or repair. But what is even more damaging to the authentic age ascribed by tradition is the presence near its center of a bead which shows up opaque like a metal object on the x-ray plate, and is presumably made of lead glass, which must have reached Onondaga in colonial times. It appears to have been incorporated in the belt when it was first woven and not inserted afterward. We do not know whether or how belts were repaired, although several appear to have added beads at the margins. Just how this was done awaits further work. I suspect that the design itself is as old as the League, that the present belt is not the original, and again I agree with Beauchamp that the present belt dates from the mid-eighteenth century when purple wampum became abundant.[95]

Aided by x-ray technology, Fenton felt he was able to accurately date the Aionwà:tha belt and the other two "Great Belts of the League," the Atotárho and the Ever-growing Tree:

I place these last three belts in the same period, the middle decades of the eighteenth century, when forest diplomacy was a great drama played between the Six Nations and His Majesty's Indian Superintendent, Sir William Johnson, the Penns, and the other colonial governors, at a time when Iroquois belts are known to be "mostly black Wampum..." and "...they describe Castles [towns] sometimes upon them as square figures of White Wampum". The symbolism, in my opinion, is much older than the belts themselves.[96]

I was intrigued by this "lead glass bead" in the Aionwà:tha belt, so I contacted my friend at the New York State Museum, George Hamell, for further information.

Yes, there is a white, high lead content glass (trade) bead woven into the Hiawatha Belt. It is so similar in superficial appearance to the white wampum beads adjacent to it that it is very difficult to visually distinguish it. You really have to be pointed to it and then note the differences in surface appearance between it and the neighboring white wampum beads. However, because of its high lead content it fluoresces under x-ray and is easily distinguished in the x-ray of the Hiawatha Belt. Fenton reported it in 1971, and I relocated it in 1987 as I prepared the twelve wampum belts for return to Onondaga. The white glass bead appears in the pictograph either representing the Cayuga — if the belt is viewed such as the Great Tree appears in the middle — or representing the Oneida — if the belt is viewed such as the "heart" appears in the middle of the belt.

The glass bead probably is contemporary with the date of the wampum beads comprising the belt. I could accept a date of 1660-1670 for the Hiawatha Belt's creation based upon the consistency of the wampum beads' sizes and proportions, and drilling (with metal tools) techniques. I believe William M. Beauchamp thought it more recent and composed of beads that he called "council wampum," a description whose meaning escapes me.

The belt obviously postdates the Iroquois Confederacy's founding, but undoubtedly commemorates it, and was prepared by someone having access to "new" wampum beads of consistent quality, size, and proportion. "New" that is in the third quarter of the 17th century.[97]

In his 1998 *The Great Law and the Longhouse*, Fenton stood by his estimate that the Aionwà:tha belt was made in Molly Brant's era, the late 1700's, while Hamell posited the belt in the time of *Kateri Tekakwitha*, a century or so earlier.[98] Both agreed that the Aionwà:tha belt was made at the same time as the Atotárho and the Ever-growing Tree.

While the Aionwà:tha belt may not have originated in the time of the confederacy's founding, it certainly memorializes that event, and we can forgive the chiefs for assuming it was much older. In their defense, they carried a lot of information in their heads, including the league tradition itself, which could take several days to recite properly, not to mention the songs, ceremonies, and day-to-day knowledge of Indian life.

Today the belt itself is back in the hands of the Rotinonhsón:ni Confederacy after a prolonged stay at the New York State Museum. The three "Great Belts of the League" were repatriated by the Grand Council in 1989, along with a number of other historic belts in the museum's collection. The Onondaga wampum keepers zealously guard access to it, and were even opposed to using its imagery as the basis of an Iroquois flag, but this did not prevent the people from adopting it as their universal symbol. Eventually they too would place orders for the "unofficial" flag and are now flying it proudly.

19

THE *ATOTÁRHO* BELT: PRESIDENTIA OF THE IROQUOIS

The Atotárho is the second of the three "Great Belts of the League." Like the Ever-growing Tree, it isn't as well known as the Aionwà:tha belt, but it is an important part of the league tradition.

For the story behind this belt, we turn again to Thomas and Daniel La Fort and William Beauchamp, our sources for the Aionwà:tha belt tradition. Daniel and Thomas La Fort told E. W. Paige that the belt represented:

> ...a superior man—To-do-da-ho. That is a carpet for him to sit. You clean the carpet for him to sit and nothing evil can fall on the carpet. They have furnished two prominent women and having a broom so that it would be clean. This was in the lifetime of To-do-da-ho, and the Five Nations furnish him a stick, laying close by where he sits—represents as a limited power given to him by the Five Nations. If he sees something evil coming he would take the stick and throw away, and if the stick

not strong enough then he would notify the Five Nations to come help him; that the animal and wild peoples come prepared for war. The *To-do-da-ho* would speak to the animal and ask: What is thy business coming here without our knowledge?[99]

Beauchamp described the Atotárho belt as

...another modern belt of the same date, termed by Mr Donaldson, "Presidentia of the Iroquois, about 1540." A series of dark points inclose open white diamonds, signifying nations or towns. It is properly a chain belt, showing a completed covenant. When Gen. Carrington photographed it in 1890, it had lost nothing since first seen by the writer. Before it again came into the latter's hands it had been reduced from 16 to 14 diamonds. It is 45 rows wide or 13.5 inches, and was incomplete in length when examined in 1878. The material is as in the last, and both seem to have been made by one person. The note of 1886 says, "The first belt used by the principal chief of the Six Nations. Very old." Both these were secured for the state in 1898, and they are the broadest on record. Unique in every way their modern origin is at once apparent to any careful observer, but no definite date can be given them...[100]

The late Leon Shenandoah held the title of Atotárho (*Tadodaho* in Onondaga) from 1969 until his death in 1996. Steve Wall interviewed him for a book that was published after he died, *To Become a Human Being: The Message of Tadodaho Chief Leon Shenandoah* (2001). Shenanodah had this to say about his namesake, the evil wizard of Onondaga:

Let me tell you about the original Tadodaho. To understand, you have to go back to when they found him. It was thick with woods where he lived. It seems that it was in a gully where they found him. In a gully! He was lying on the ground with seven women. They were all Hiawatha's daughters and they were dead. It says they found seven girls lying there. I don't know if they took him or what, but he had this "thing" over his shoulder. Maybe that's what killed them. His "thing" was so long he had it over his shoulder. He must have used it like a club for it to have killed those women.

The word Tadodaho means in translation, "Snakes Entangled." When they first found him his hair was all messed up. It looked like snakes coming out of there. That's when the Peacemaker saw and felt with all those snakes that the Tadodaho must be evil. He was so evil! All of the people were afraid of Tadodaho because he was so mean and evil. He was the most feared one of all even though the other leaders were all feared by the people, too. The Peacemaker looked for the evil ones. The Peacemaker knew that if they were reformed they would make good leaders. His mission on Earth was to reform them for the good of the people. Once he found them, they weren't evil when he left them. They were gentle then. When the Peacemaker reformed the leaders, even the Tadodaho, he gave them the Instructions. That was the beginning of the Five Nations Confederacy. It became Six Nations when the Tuscarora joined after being pushed out of what is now North Carolina. Because the Peacemaker changed the original Tadodaho to start working for the benefit of his people, after he died, the people used his name as the title of the highest position in the Confederacy. Nobody knows how many leaders have held the position of Tadodaho. It's talked in the Longhouse that there have been over fifty in the last one thousand years. Once selected, you hold the office for life unless you start working for yourself and not the people. The chiefs can be removed for that. Since I became Tadodaho in 1969 I have done my best and worked for only the good.[101]

Shenandoah was present when the Atotárho belt and other wampums were returned to the Rotinonhsón:ni by the New York State Museum in 1989. Today his title is held by Sid Hill, the latest in a long line of men who have served the people in that capacity.

20

THE EVER-GROWING TREE BELT: A PROPHECY IN WAMPUM

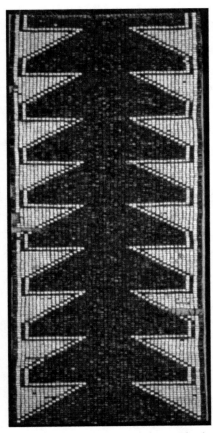

The third of the "great belts" is known by three names, the Ever-growing Tree, the Wing, and the Dust Fan. Some call it the Fan Belt for short, but this inevitably leads to jokes about how they must have had really big engines in the old days and how mad the women were about having to making a new wampum belt every ten or twenty thousand miles.

William Beauchamp knew that wampum was serious business. This is what he said about the belt in question:

...represents the widest belt known, one of 50 rows wide. Through a slight mistake of the writer this was reported to Mr Holmes as 49 rows. It is 14.75 inches wide and about 35 inches long. Though not of the original length it has not been diminished since it was first pictured. The pattern is decidedly modern as well as the material. It is made on small buckskin thongs with a hard, red thread. The interpretation of 1886 was, "The second belt used by the principal chief of the Six Nations. Very old." Mr T. Donaldson's note is similar. He calls it "Wing or Dust Fan of Presidentia of Six Nations." Also "the wing mat used by the head man to shield him from the dust, while presiding at the council." It seems to represent an alliance actual or proposed, and to be of the variety termed chain belts.[102]

Thomas and Daniel La Fort gave a completely different interpretation in 1898:

Represents an everlasting tree—always keep growing, reaching to heaven that all nations may see it; and under they set a general fire to burn forever—the council place of the Five Nations—and that the council fire is to be kept at the Onondagas, and the Onondagas are the expounders of the law.

After they had ratified—it was understood—we look far away and we see a darkness, and in the darkness an unknown and strange face, and they could not understand what it was— and it came to be interpreted that we would be forced to adopt an unknown law but it was coming before that generation passed away, and finally their heads would roll and roll away, and after a time they would recover their bodies, and then they would embrace the law that was once lost to them, and the tree would grow forever. After they will restore the original law their confederation will be more permanent than the first one, and their original law will remain forever. They say that one of the women said: "You can use all the water of the ocean to wash away the Indian blood, and when you have done there is just as much water left in the ocean as before you began—so the law—you can take from it parts of the Indian law, and put another in its place, but it will come again and last forever."

This was the last belt that was made at that ratifying time. When the belt was ready it was said by one of the orators to that council, "This is the last belt which we make confirming the laws which we have just adopted," and he encouraged the people of the Five Nations to instruct them with the meaning of the wampum to serve the laws. At the conclusion of his remarks he said: "As long as you will follow up the laws of the Five Nations you will be in prosperity and happiness, but whenever our people may not heed the instructions which we instructing to you, then it will come in the state of dissension among our people—and the last remark—if you will disobey and disregard the laws we have, that generation will suffer. *Hi-a-wat-ha* made that speech. This belt is not the original which was there at that time, but a copy. It was made not a great while after the death of *Hi-a-wat-ha*. That each clan shall be entitled to one principal chief and war chief. When the council ended, *Hi-a-wat-ha* went up the Onondaga creek and distributed the belts among the clans, making the clans and chiefs. And in his speech he said: "I have made a place for you under ground and a fishing ground. I have finished my work." It is claimed that he did not die, but went up in his canoe and said: "When you shall be in a state of confusion I will come back."

That *Hi-a-wat-ha* saw the strange face in the midst of the darkness, and he interpreted it that the unknown law which was coming, should prevail over the new law—that is, the law which has just been adopted and the tree that was just planted. The root spread from east to west, and from south to north. Under the tree, while the root of the tree was spreading, all the Five Nations laid their heads on the root. That is the constitution. If any of their enemies should attempt to strike against the root—from their enemies destroying some of their people, and after striking against up the root, the man who struck the root would turn, and the blood would come out of his mouth. That is revenge for blood. The roots of the tree would continue spreading in all directions forever; and the fire would continue forever, and the smoke of it go all up to heaven, so that all the nations of the world would see; and that the laws—that is the wampums—be read every year forever...

...*Hi-a-wat-ha* would come again, but when he did not say. He did not die, and when he came again he would renew the old, and it would be stronger than then, and that is the expectation we have. The former meetings of the Five Nations were on Onondaga lake, and some near Liverpool. He was the proclaimer of councils, and the only proper person to call a council. These wampums were made during these meetings, and were complete at the last meeting when everything was ratified.[103]

The La Fort interpretation emphasizes Aionwà:tha as the mystic founder of the Five Nations, which is consistent with the Onondaga league traditions recorded in the previous century. It also warns of a coming "dark time," when the ancient league of Aionwà:tha would be overtaken by a "new law."

These words have proven prophetic so far. They were recorded over a century ago, when there was growing pressure on the Iroquois to adopt elections. They may have been talking about their own times, but the same applies today, with elected and traditional forms of government vying for legitimacy.

In spite of the "darkness" that would one day befall the Iroquois, Aionwà:tha tells us that his league will ultimately rise up again, and become even stronger than before, like an ever-growing tree with roots that continue to grow to the ends of the earth.

21

RAIDERS OF THE STONE CANOE

It has never been my intention to disprove or challenge anyone's treasured beliefs by presenting the differences between the various versions of our creation story and the confederation epic, or by documenting their evolution over the years. To acknowledge that the stories have evolved over time, and to speculate about the historicity of the events they portray, has been as much a matter of faith to me as it would be for someone else to accept them without question.

The stories of creation and confederation are evolving traditions, something as alive as we are. As such there is no definitive version of either of these tales, anymore than there could ever be a definitive human being.

That they have been written down over the years does not diminish their legitimacy as oral traditions. A written literature was being created, but very few of the keepers of these traditions had access to it, scattered as it was in archives and libraries. That's why each recorded example of these legends is of such value to us today, because they allow us to tap into "pure" oral tradition at various points in history.

When we consider how endangered our language and culture have become, it is not surprising to find fundamentalist interpretations about our culture among modern Rotinonhsón:ni. When we take things too literally, however, we run the risk of missing the subtle truths laying just below the surface. Likewise, when we focus on only one version of the Great Law of Peace, we miss out on the story that reveals itself when you lay all of the different versions end to end. We miss the story behind the story—our own evolution.

Fundamentalism tends to polarize a community. This was true when Seth Newhouse and the Six Nations chiefs committee split hairs about *The Good Message of Peace, Power and Righteousness* more than a century ago. Dogmatic interpretations of our culture were also at the heart of the civil conflicts at Ahkwesáhsne, Kahnawà:ke, and Kanehsatà:ke in more recent times. They're the reason why we have multiple longhouses springing up in our territories—and increasing division between our elected and traditional leaders.

I do not believe that our traditions lend themselves to such extreme interpretations. When we become divided over a message meant to inspire unity, we have truly reached the "dark times" predicted by Aionwà:tha, when the heads of the people would "roll and roll away" in a state of confusion. Now is the time to recover our bodies and embrace the law that was once lost to us.

In the end, it doesn't really matter if the Peacemaker was a Huron mystic from the Bay of Quinte or a Mohawk chief from the Mohawk Valley—or if he wasn't Tekanawí:ta at all but the wandering Onondaga, Aionwà:tha. Nor does it matter if his canoe was made of stone. What does matter is what we do with the message these men have brought before us. Do we accept it as something we can actually use and live by, or is it just another high-minded body of teachings that nobody can possibly live up to? Are we free to create something new from it that we can use? "The prophet who is to succeed among the Iroquois must use the old words and relate his program to old ways," wrote William Fenton. "He is a conservator at the same time that he is a reformer."[104]

I will leave you with a final story, this one from the pouch of my own "living history," which will remain the final word on the subject...at least as far as this book goes.

I mentioned earlier that I spent a summer selling T-shirts at powwows. At one event in Montreal several years back, I was approached by a Mohawk woman from Tyendinaga, the Mohawk community on the Bay of Quinte—yes, *that* Bay of Quinte, the traditional birthplace of the Peacemaker. Since retired French-Canadians don't often buy T-shirts that say *Jacques Cartier Was a Scurvy Dog*, we had time to have a nice chat about Mohawk history.

This woman, whose name I will keep to myself, told me a story about an old man she knew, whose name she kept to herself. This man was boating on a river in the Bay of Quinte area and found what he thought was a petroglyph on a rock jutting out of the riverbank. On further inspection, he realized that it wasn't just a rock, but what appeared to be the prow of a stone canoe. When he told someone about his discovery, the people he told it to only laughed at him. Apparently, this old man wasn't Longhouse and didn't know the tradition of the Peacemaker's stone canoe. Being laughed at apparently wasn't one of his favorite traditions, either, so he kept it to himself after that.

Somehow this woman found out about it, and told it to me. I later attempted to track this story down in the hopes of going out to find this alleged stone canoe, but nothing ever materialized. Knowing me, if I ever did find it, I would probably dig a little deeper and find out it was just a weird rock shaped like the prow of a canoe that somebody decided to paint on. So perhaps it is better left unfound, where it can continue to exist in the realm of the living culture—awaiting the moment when we call out the sacred name of the Peacemaker into the forests, bidding his return.

NOTES

1   This name is usually rendered in it's Onondaga form, *Haudenosaunee*.

2   Snow, D. R., C. T. Gehring, W. A. Starna, ed. *In Mohawk Country: Early Narratives about a Native People*. Syracuse University Press. Syracuse. 1996:45-46.

3   Hislop, Codman. *The Mohawk*. New York/Toronto: Rinehart & Company, Inc. 1948:15.

4   Snow, D. R. "Mohawk Valley Archaeology: the Sites." *Occasional Papers in Anthropology*. Matson Museum of Anthropology, The Pennsylvania State University, University Park. no. 23. 1995:199.

5   Snow, D. R., C. T. Gehring, W. A. Starna, ed. *In Mohawk Country: Early Narratives about a Native People*. Syracuse University Press. Syracuse. 1996:129-130.

6   Snow, *Mohawk*, 52.

7   Snow, *Mohawk*, 45.

8   Mitchell, M. K. "The Origin of Man." *Traditional Teachings*. North American Indian Travelling College. Ahkwesáhsne. 1984. 7-8.

9   NASA Website. http://science.nasa.gov/headlines/y2005/29jul_planetx.htm?list109322. Text cited from content of August 8, 2005.

10   *The Official Website of Zecharia Sitchin*. http://www.sitchin.com. Text cited from content of August 8, 2005.

11   Lafitau, J. F. *Customs of the American Indians Compared with the Customs of Primitive Times*. The Champlain Society, Toronto. vol. I, 1974:81-82.

12   Lafitau, *Customs*, I, 82-83.

13   Lafitau, *Customs*, I, 84.

14   Lafitau, *Customs*, I, 85.

15   Lafitau, *Customs*, I, 85.

16   Lafitau, *Customs*, I, 85.

17   Lafitau, *Customs*, I, 82.

18   Fenton, W. N. "Joseph-Francois Lafitau." *Dictionary of Canadian Biography Online*. As found at http://www.biographi.ca/EN/ShowBio.asp?BioId=35558

19   Klink, C. F., J. T. Talman, ed. *The Journal of Major John Norton, 1816*. The Champlain Society, Toronto. 1970:91.

20   Hewitt, J. N. B. *Iroquoian Cosmology*. AMS Press. New York. 1974.

21   Blanchard, D. *Seven Generations*. Kahnawake Survival School. Kahnawà:ke. 1980.

22   Myers, M. "The Sky World." *Traditional Teachings*. North American Indian Travelling College. Ahkwesáhsne. 1984:5-6.

23   George, D. M., Shenandoah, J. *Skywoman: Legends of the Iroquois.* Clear Light
      Publishers, Santa Fe. 1998.

24   Mohawk, J. C. *Iroquois Creation Story: John Arthur Gibson and J. N. B. Hewitt's
      Myth of the Earth Grasper.* Mohawk Publications, Buffalo. 2005.

25   Parker, A. C. "Emblematic Trees in Iroquoian Mythology," *Seneca Myths and Folk
      Tales.* Buffalo Historical Society, Buffalo. 1923:433-434.

26   Parker, *Seneca,* 435-436.

27   Parker, *Seneca,* 436.

28   Parker, *Seneca,* 431.

29   Lafitau, *Customs,* I, 86.

30   Lighthall, W. D. "Hochelagans and Mohawks; A Link in Iroquois History."
      Transactions of the Royal Society of Canada, 1899:208 Lighthall cites François-
      Xavier de Charlevoix's 1744 *Histoire et description générale de la Nouvelle-France
      (History and general description of Nouvelle-France).*

31   Schoolcraft, H. R. *Notes on the Iroquois: or, Contributions to the Statistics,
      Aboriginal History, Antiquities and General Ethnology of Western New-York.* Bartlett
      & Welford, Astor House. New York. 1846: 39-40. Edition cited: Kraus Reprint
      Co. Millwood. 1975.

32   Beauchamp, W. M. *The Iroquois Trail, or Foot-prints of the Six Nations in Customs,
      Traditions, and History.* H. C. Beauchamp, Recorder Office, Fayetteville. 1892:5.

33   Beauchamp, *Iroquois,* 10.

34   Beauchamp, *Iroquois,* 10-11.

35   Rice, B. Personal communication. January 6, 2005.

36   Thwaites, R. G. *The Jesuit Relations and Allied Documents,
      1610-1791.* Cleveland: Burrows Bros:1896-1901. vol. 42:252.

37   Tooker, E. "The League of the Iroquois: Its History, Politics, and Ritual."
      Handbook of North American Indians. vol. 15 Northeast. 1978:418-422.

38   Fenton, W. N. *The Great Law and the Longhouse: A Political History of the Iroquois
      Confederacy.* University of Oklahoma Press, Norman. 1998:53.

39   Fenton, *Great,* 53-54.

40   Hewitt, J. N. B. "Era of the Formation of the Historic League of the Iroquois."
      The American Anthropologist. vol. 7. 1894.

41   Fenton, *Great,* 71.

42   Fenton, Great, 71.

43   Mann, B. A., J. L. Fields. "A Sign in the Sky: Dating the League of the
      Haudenosaunee." *American Indian Culture and Research Journal.* vol. 21:2.
      1987:136.

44 Snow, D. R. "Dating the Emergence of the League of the Iroquois: A Reconstruction of the Documentary Evidence." *Selected Rensselaerswijck Seminar Papers*, September, 1982:139-143.

45 Mann, *Sign*, 105-163.

46 Fenton, *Great*, 71.

47 *The Jesuit Relations and Allied Documents*. vol. 39: 143. Text cited from http://puffin.creighton.edu/jesuit/relations/relations_39.html.

48 *The Jesuit Relations and Allied Documents*. vol. 58:180-183. Text cited from http://puffin.creighton.edu/jesuit/relations/relations_58.html.

49 Wall, S. *To Become a Human Being: The Message of Tadodaho Chief Leon Shenandoah*. Hampton Roads Publishing Company, Inc. Charlottsville. 2001:6.

50 Dennis, M. *Cultivating a Landscape of Peace: Iroquois-European Encounters in Seventeenth-Century America*. Cornell University Press. Ithica. 1993:52-63.

51 Grumet, R. S. *Historic Contact: Indian People and Colonists in Today's Northeastern United States in the Sixteenth Through Eighteenth Centuries*. University of Oklahoma Press. Norman and London. 1995:377. Snow believes the Oneidas were an offshoot of the Mohawks, while others believe they were originally Onondagas.

52 Boyce, D. W. "A Glimpse of Iroquois Culture History Through the Eyes of Joseph Brant and John Norton." *Proceedings of the American Philosophical Society*. vol. 117:4 August 1973:288-289

53 Beauchamp, W. M. *Iroquois Folk Lore Gathered From the Six Nations of New York*. The Dehler Press, Syracuse. 1922. Edition cited: Empire State Historical Publication XXXI. Ira J. Friedman, Inc. Port Washington. (no date) 67.

54 Klink, *Journal*.

55 Klink, *Journal*, 98-100.

56 Klink, Journal, 100.

57 *Catholic Family Edition of the Holy Bible*. John J. Crawley & Co., Inc. New York. 1953. John 4:44.

58 Klink, *Journal*, 100-102.

59 Klink, *Journal*, 102-105.

60 Schoolcraft, H. B. *Information Concerning the History, Condition and Prospects of the Indian Tribes of the United States*. Lippincott, Grambo & Company, Philadelphia. Part III. 1853:314-315.

61 Schoolcraft, *Information*, 315-316.

62 Schoolcraft, *Information*, 316.

63 Schoolcraft, *Information*, 316-317.

64   Hale, H. E. *The Iroquois Book of Rites and Hale on the Iroquois*. Iroquois Reprint Series. Iroqrafts, Ohswé:ken. 1989:24-25.

65   Hale, *Iroquois*, 31-32.

66   Fenton, W. N. "Seth Newhouse's Traditional History and Constitution of the Iroquois Confederacy." *Proceedings of the American Philosophical Society*. vol. 93:2. May, 1949:152.

67   Scott, D. C. "Traditional History of the Confederacy of the Six Nations, Prepared by a Committee of the Chiefs." *Transactions of the Royal Society of Canada*, 3d. ser. 5(2). Royal Society of Canada, Ottawa. 1912:195-246.

68   Parker, A. C. *Parker on the Iroquois*. Syracuse University Press, Syracuse. 1968.

69   Parker, A. C. "The Constitution of the Five Nations, or the Iroquois Book of the Great Law." *New York State Museum Bulletin*. no. 184. April 1, 1916. Iroquois Reprint Series. Iroqrafts, Ohswé:ken. 1991:65-66.

70   Parker, *Constitution*, 66-68.

71   Parker, *Constitution*, 15.

72   Mitchell, M. K. "The Birth of the Peacemaker." *Traditional Teachings*. North American Indian Travelling College, Ahkwesáhsne. 1984:17.

73   Woodbury, H. *Concerning the League: The Iroquois League Tradition as Dictated in Onondaga by John Arthur Gibson*. Algonquin and Iroquoian Linguistics Memo 9. Winnipeg. 1992:1-2.

74   Parker, *Constitution*, 62-63.

75   Mann, *Sign*, 114.

76   Gabriel-Doxtator, B. K. *At the Woods' Edge: An Anthology of the History of the People of Kanehsatake*. Kanehsatake Education Centre, Kanehsatà:ke. 1995:39.

77   Hansen, L. T. *He Walked the Americas*. Amherst Press, Amherst. 1963: 61-65.

78   Schoolcraft, *Information*, 315.

79   Fenton, *Great*, 69.

80   Heidenreich, C. E. "Huron." *Handbook of North American Indians*. vol. 15 Northeast. 1978:368-369.

81   Parker, *Constitution*: 172.

82   Klink, *Journal*, 105-107.

83   Leland, C. G. *The Algonquin Legends of New England or Myths and Folk Lore of the Micmac, Passamaquoddy, and Penobscot Tribes*. The Riverside Press, Cambridge, 1884. As found online at http://www.sacred-texts.com/nam/ne/al/al40.htm.

84   Beauchamp, *Iroquois*, 144-146.

85   Parker, A. C. *Seneca Myths and Folk Tales*. Buffalo Historical Society, Buffalo. 1923: 403-406.

86   Hewitt, J. N. B. *American Anthropologist* (New Series), vol. 19, no. 3, 1917:436. As quoted in Parker, A. C., *The Constitution of the Five Nations or The Iroquois Book of the Great Law*, Iroquois Reprints Series, Iroqrafts, Ohswé:ken, 1991:174-175.

87   Leland, *Algonquin*, 15-18. As found online at http://www.sacred-texts.com/nam/ne/al/al06.htm.

88   Leland, *Algonquin*, 127-130. As found online at http://www.sacred-texts.com/nam/ne/al/al30.htm.

89   Found online at http://collections.ic.gc.ca/virtualtours/eskbird.html.

90   Found online at http://www.absoluteastronomy.com/encyclopedia/a/ab/abenaki_mythology.htm.

91   Found online at http://groups.msn.com/asinglestandingteepee/nativestoies.msnw.

92   Beauchamp, W. M. "Wampum and Shell Articles Used by the New York Indians." *Bulletin of the New York State Museum.* no. 41 February 1901:410.

93   Beauchamp, *Wampum*, 420.

94   Beauchamp, *Wampum*, 411-412.

95   Fenton, W. N. "The New York State Wampum Collection: The Case for the Integrity of Cultural Treasures." *Proceedings of the American Philosophical Society.* vol. 115:6 December 1971:443-446.

96   Fenton, *Proceedings*, 446.

97   Hamell, G. Personal communication, December 22, 2003.

98   Fenton, *Great*, 236.

99   Beauchamp, *Wampum*, 419-420.

100 Beauchamp, *Wampum*, 412.

101 Wall, *Become*, 5-6.

102 Beauchamp, *Wampum*, 412

103 Beauchamp, *Wampum*, 420-421

104 Fenton, *Great*, 36.

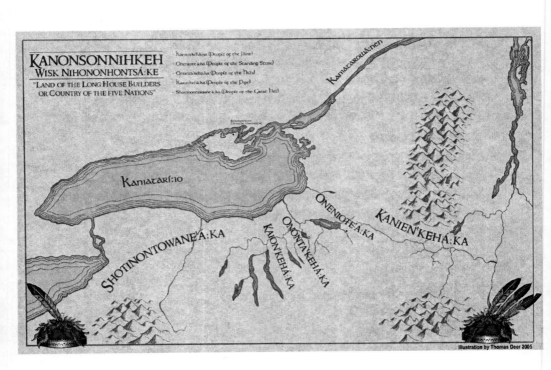

KANONSONNIHKEH
WISK NIHONONHONTSÁ:KE

"LAND OF THE LONG HOUSE BUILDERS
OR COUNTRY OF THE FIVE NATIONS"

Kanien'kehá:ka (People of the Flint)
Onenioteá:ka (People of the Standing Stone)
Ononta'kehá:ka (People of the Hills)
Kaionkehá:ka (People of the Pipe)
Shotinontowane'á:ka (People of the Great Hill)

Kaniataróuàs:nen

Kaniatarí:io

SHOTINONTOWANE'Á:KA

KAIONKEHÁ:KA

ONONTA'KEHÁ:KA

ONENIOTEÁ:KA

KANIEN'KEHÁ:KA

Illustration by Thomas Deer 2005